PRAISE FOR

Heart of a Competitor™

Athletics can be a great way to learn lessons about everyday life.
But what is really special is when you can take athletic lessons and
apply them to your spiritual life. *Heart of a Competitor* takes a look at how
the tests we face as players and coaches can help us grow as Christians.

Coach Tony Dungy
Former Head Coach, Indianapolis Colts

In the *Heart of a Competitor,* you will see that it is just as important
to train spiritually as it is to train physically and mentally. When you focus
on training the total body, it will take you to the next level.

Tamika Catchings
WNBA Player and Four-term Olympic Gold Medalist

Having a competitive nature obviously affects things on the pitching
mound, but it also translates into life off the mound. As believers, we are
called to work with all of our hearts, as though working for the Lord and
not for man (see Colossians 3:23). That means baseball, and that means life.
Heart of a Competitor is an awesome resource for believers—both on and off
the field. Each devotional is an encouragement to live and compete for the
Lord's glory. Life isn't always about winning a game; it's about living for the
Lord in all that we do. This book helps to keep that in perspective.

Clayton Kershaw
Major League Baseball Pitcher and Co-author of *Arise*
National League Cy Young Award Winner (2011)
Roberto Clemente Award Winner (2012)

HEART
OF A
COMPETITOR™

Regal

For more information and
special offers from Regal Books, email us at
subscribe@regalbooks.com

Published by Regal
From Gospel Light
Ventura, California, U.S.A.
www.regalbooks.com
Printed in the U.S.A.

All Scripture quotations, unless otherwise indicated, are taken from the *Holman Christian Standard Bible.* © 2001, Broadman and Holman Publishers, Lifeway Christian Resources, 127 Ninth Avenue North, Nashville, TN 37234.

Other versions used are
NIV—Scripture taken from the *Holy Bible, New International Version*®. Copyright © 1973, 1978, 1984, 2010 by International Bible Society. Used by permission of Zondervan Publishing House. All rights reserved.
NKJV—Scripture taken from the *New King James Version.* Copyright © 1979, 1980, 1982 by Thomas Nelson, Inc. Used by permission. All rights reserved.
NLT—Scripture quotations marked *NLT* are taken from the *Holy Bible, New Living Translation,* copyright © 1996, 2004, 2007 by Tyndale House Foundation. Used by permission of Tyndale House Publishers, Inc., Carol Stream, Illinois 60188. All rights reserved.

Dan Britton, General Editor.
Shea Vailes, Contributing Editor.

Rights for publishing this book outside the U.S.A. or in non-English languages are administered by Gospel Light Worldwide, an international not-for-profit ministry. For additional information, please visit www.glww.org, email info@glww.org, or write to Gospel Light Worldwide, 1957 Eastman Avenue, Ventura, CA 93003, U.S.A.

To order copies of this book and other Regal products in bulk quantities, please contact us at 1-800-446-7735.

Contents

Letter from the President

Dear Teammate:

The mark of a true competitor is found in the heart. Here is where every competitive passion begins and where our relationship with God is grown. These 90 devotionals are written from a competitor's mindset and include Bible verses to help you understand God's perspective on key issues. Our hope is that this book will motivate you to develop a consistent, focused way of spending time with God so you will deepen your understanding of His Word and become a true competitor for Jesus Christ.

As a competitor, you have been given a tremendous platform from which to influence others. We pray that God will use these devotions to transform your life as a competitor so that you can make an eternal impact for Jesus Christ.

Your Teammate in Christ,

Les Steckel

Les Steckel
FCA President/CEO

Introduction

Training Time

In sports, time-outs give athletes and coaches a chance to strategize for upcoming challenges. Similarly, in life, we need to take time-outs to think about our purpose as members of God's team. FCA is excited to present you with a collection of devotions that will challenge you to play and live for the glory of God. Each devotion is written from an athletic perspective and will encourage you to be more like Christ both on and off the field.

Every morning, set aside a special quiet time to be with God. During this spiritual training time, talk to God and let Him speak to you through the Bible. There are many effective methods that can be used for your daily time with God. One method that we recommend is the PRESS method.

The PRESS Method

Pray

Begin your quiet time by thanking God for the new day, and then ask Him to help you learn from what you read. Prepare yourself by:

- clearing your mind and being quiet before the Lord
- asking God to settle your heart
- listening to worship music to prepare your spirit
- asking God to give you a teachable heart

Read

Begin with the 90 devotionals provided in this book. Also, try reading a chapter of Proverbs every day (there are 31 chapters in Proverbs, which makes it ideal for daily reading), one psalm and/or a chapter out of the Old or New Testament. You may consider beginning with one of the Gospels (Matthew, Mark, Luke or John), or one of the shorter letters such as Ephesians or James.

Examine

Ask yourself the following questions in regard to the passage you read:

- *Teaching:* What do I need to *know* about God, myself and others?
- *Rebuking:* What do I need to *stop* doing—sins, habits, selfish patterns?
- *Correcting:* What do I need to *change* in my thoughts, attitudes or actions?
- *Training:* What do I need to *do* in obedience to God's leading?

Summarize

Do one of the following:

- Discover what the passage reveals about God and His character, what it says or promises about you, and what it says or promises about others (such as your parents, friends or teammates). Write your thoughts down in a personal journal.
- Rewrite one or two key verses in your own words.
- Outline what each verse is saying.
- Give each verse a one-word title that summarizes what it says.

Share

Talk with God about what you've learned. Also, take time each day to share with someone what you learned during that day's study. Having a daily training time is the key to spiritual development. If you commit to working through these 90 devotionals over the next three months, you will establish this as a habit—one that will be vital to your growth in Christ. If you are committed to establishing this daily training time with God, fill out the box below.

I will commit to establishing this daily habit.

Signed _____ Today's Date _____

Writers

We have assembled athletes, coaches and team chaplains from all levels (in addition to FCA staff) to contribute their time, talent and experience in writing these devotions. These writers come from diverse backgrounds and include representatives from a variety of sports, including baseball, soccer, basketball, football, lacrosse, track and field, and others.

Format

Ready   A verse or passage from Scripture that focuses or directs your heart and mind. Turn to the Scripture reference in your Bible and read it within the overall context of the passage.

Set   A teaching point (a story, training point or thought taken from a sports perspective) that draws a lesson from the passage.

Go   Questions that will help you examine your heart and challenge you to apply God's truth to your life—on and off the field.

Workout   Additional scripture references to help you dig deeper.

Overtime   A closing prayer that will help you commit to the Lord what you have learned.

**To receive the daily e-mail devotional
"FCA's Impact Play," go to www.FCA.org.**

1

What's Your Purpose?

Ready

The LORD will fulfill His purpose for me. LORD, Your love is eternal; do not abandon the work of Your hands.

PSALM 138:8

Set

I've been in the Major Leagues for more than 10 years with the Baltimore Orioles. Looking back I can think of specific guys who were crucial to my development and maturity as a person and a baseball player. Now, as a veteran, I feel that it's my role to share what I've learned from my experiences in the same way guys did with me when I was younger.

Just like David says in Psalm 138, I know the Lord has a purpose for me, and He will fulfill it. I've tried over the years to grow in the understanding of my purpose. As a Christian competitor, I try to use every opportunity I can to share the gospel of Christ along with the struggles I've faced and the lessons God has taught me along the way. I have realized that my purpose goes far beyond just playing the game of baseball. God has purposed this sport as my mission field.

We've all been put here by God to be lights for Him, and we've each been given our unique gifts. It is up to us to recognize those gifts and use them for God's glory. We must be willing to use our sport, no matter the level of competition, to fulfill His purposes and to share the amazing gift of His love and grace. It should be our ultimate goal to have those around us—teammates, coaches, fans—see Christ in how we perform within our sport.

And even though we will make mistakes, sometimes secretively and other times in front of the whole world, God's grace is sufficient enough to pick us up and continue to use us for His purposes. His plans are larger than our faults, and He will always fulfill the purpose He has set for us. Never forget, His love and mercies endure forever. —*Brian Roberts*

Go

1. What do you feel is your God-given purpose? How does that purpose apply to your athletic or coaching career?
2. Have you ever felt that your inadequacies limited God's purpose for your life? What are some Scriptures that refute that belief?
3. How can you encourage others to pursue and fulfill God's purpose in their lives?

Workout

Psalm 19; Hosea 14:9; 1 Corinthians 3:1-11

Overtime

Almighty Father, You've given us each a specific purpose in this life. Let it be our passion to find that purpose and share Your saving message through it. As competitors and coaches, allow us to never take the position of influence we have been given for granted. Let it always be an honor to point people to You and Your glory. Amen.

Journal

_____

_____

_____

_____

_____

_____

_____

_____

_____

_____

_____

_____

_____

2

Overcome Adversity

Ready

No, in all these things we are more than victorious
through Him who loved us.

ROMANS 8:37

Set

As a child, I dealt with the embarrassment of having to wear glasses
and braces. And to make matters worse, I had problems with my hearing which required me to wear a hearing aid and affected my speech.
You can imagine the name-calling that ensued. I remember one day on
the way home from school, I was so frustrated that I took off my hearing aid and threw it into a ditch. Needless to say, my parents weren't
too happy about that.

By the time I was in middle school, my parents divorced and added
another layer of adversity to my life. I used sports as an escape from my
problems. But even there, I faced my share of difficulties. Throughout
my career I've torn my ACL, my meniscus and my Achilles tendon.
When I faced those tough times, it would have been easy to give up and
say, "Woe is me!" But I represent God in everything I do, and I knew
He had a plan for my life. And through those injuries and struggles,
I've drawn closer to the Lord.

God has a plan for everyone and once you've discovered that plan,
no one but you can stop it from coming to pass. This has certainly
been true in my life. I have personally experienced what it means to be
"victorious through Him who loved us." And all of the things I've experienced have given me a platform to inspire others and share with
them the love of God. By His grace, those adversities made me stronger
and helped me become the person that I am today. —*Tamika Catchings*

Go

1. What are some adversities that you have faced within and
outside of sports?

2. Read Romans 8:28. Are you able to see how God has used difficult situations in your life for the greater good? Explain.
3. Do you truly believe that God has a plan for your life? How might embracing His plan help you deal with life's challenges?

Workout
Romans 8:28; 2 Corinthians 4:8-9; 12:9-10; Philippians 4:12-13

Overtime
Lord, help me to see Your purpose for my life.
Give me the strength to overcome adversity that seeks
to discourage me from fulfilling Your ultimate plan.
In Your mighty name. Amen.

Journal

3

Be Courageous

Ready

Haven't I commanded you: be strong and
courageous? Do not be afraid or discouraged, for the
LORD your God is with you wherever you go.

JOSHUA 1:9

Set

As an NHL player, I've never been quick to admit my fears, but I've
definitely had them. When facing Edmonton in game seven of the
2006 Stanley Cup Finals, I was more nervous than I'd ever been in
my athletic career. Leaning on God during that game helped me find
strength to face my fears head on. We ended up winning the game
and the Stanley Cup, a first for the Carolina Hurricanes.

When our third son, Joey, was born, I dealt with a different kind
of fear. I had just been traded to Ottawa, and we were in the playoffs
at Pittsburgh. My wife Bridget went into labor, and I couldn't get
home in time for the delivery. When I got word that Joey was having
problems with his lungs, I had to rely heavily on my relationship
with the Lord to keep fear from creeping in. He gave me peace to
trust that He was taking care of my son and that everything would
be okay.

Fear is a natural reaction and something we all have to face from
time to time. But the Bible clearly tells us that we *don't* have to be
afraid when troublesome circumstances come our way. Joshua 1:9
encourages us that to conquer fear, we need to remember that God's
always with us, no matter what.

The truth is that we only give in to fear when we fail to fully
trust God. So instead of succumbing to our fears, let's courageously
acknowledge them and then take them to God in prayer. He will
faithfully give us the courage to walk through any challenge we face
within our sport, our health, our finances, our relationships and
every other aspect of our lives. —*Matt Cullen*

Go

1. When have you experienced fear? How did you handle it?
2. How is fear related to a lack of trust in God?
3. Read Joshua 1:9. What are some of God's characteristics that make it easier to overcome fear?

Workout

Psalm 23; Isaiah 41:10; Philippians 4:6

Overtime

Lord, give me courage when life's troubles come my way. Remind me of who You are so that I can be courageous and capable of facing any trying situation. Amen.

Journal

4

It's Not About You

Ready

They do everything to be observed by others. . . .
The greatest among you will be your servant.
Whoever exalts himself will be humbled, and whoever
humbles himself will be exalted.

MATTHEW 23:5,11-12

Set

As competitors, we want to be the best in everything. Being good is good, but being best is better. We want to go from *good* to *great* in every aspect of life. We have to be #1—on and off the field. Nobody remembers the loser. Second place? Seriously? We engage in the relentless pursuit of excellence!

"I must be the best me" is a principle I believe and live daily. In Luke 12:48 we are told that to whom much is entrusted, much is required. No matter what gifts you've been given, we must have a desire to be faithful and maximize them. If it's all about me, then I'll end up empty. Striving to get better in all aspects of our life isn't a bad thing. But if it's a selfish pursuit; it will never satisfy. When I live at my best, everyone else should benefit, because we are made for others.

We get—so we can give to others. We are loved—so we can love others. We are blessed—so we can bless others. We are meant to be a river, not a pond! Our purpose is to serve and bless others. Jesus takes aim at all of us who want to be great for our own selfish benefit and the applause of people.

People of impact have a three word job description: Make others better! NFL players like Tim Tebow and Ray Lewis get this. When they step into the weight room or onto the practice field, everybody gets better; their desire to be their personal best spills over onto their teammates. When they work hard, everybody else works harder.

They lead by example, challenging and encouraging everybody else to fulfill their God-given potential. They take it to a different level—intentionally mentoring the next generation of players by investing their lives in others. They model personally what they desire for others. Tebow and Lewis feel an obligation to give back, serve others and make others better. These men model the words of Jesus.

When Jesus is the center, we take our eyes off us and are willing to invest in others. Serve. Sacrifice. Give. Love. If we pursue Christ in an effort to become more like Him, we can make others better. And this only happens because of Jesus in us. Coaches and athletes, this is what we are called to do: make others better, *today*. —*Dan Britton*

Go

1. In what areas of your life are you striving to be better? Are you making progress?
2. Are you making others around you better? How so?
3. As a competitor, what ways can you intentionally serve, build up and encourage?

Workout

John 13; Philippians 2:1-11

Overtime

Lord God in Heaven, I desire to make others better. Teach me Your ways so that I can help, bless and encourage others. Show me how to put others before myself. I want to be your vessel today. In the name of Jesus I pray. Amen.

Journal

_____

_____

_____

_____

_____

_____

_____

5

First Things First

Ready

Now the end of all things is near; therefore, be serious and disciplined for prayer. Above all, maintain an intense love for each other, since love covers a multitude of sins.

1 PETER 4:7-8

Set

Part of the challenge in life is it is so daily. As a competitor, it is a battle not to treat today's practice as just one more in what feels like an endless amount. It seems the only competitors who really value each workout are those who realize there isn't an infinite amount: those returning from injury, at the end of their final season or especially those who have been told they do not have long to live. These individuals truly make each day count.

A valuable exercise is to write your own obituary. Or picture the final game of your final season, and you are asked to thank your teammates and coaches. This helps you begin with the end in mind. What would you do if you knew the end was near? The Bible tells us that the end is near, and we must do two things: be prayerful and loving toward each other. In fact, Jesus knew His death was imminent and what did He do—He prayed and His request of the Father was that His followers would be united in love (John 17).

If today were your last, you would likely be in prayer, and you would not hold back speaking and showing love to those around you. Be a leader. Your teammates and coaches will gain the courage to follow your example. What are you waiting for? —*Kerry O'Neill*

Go

1. If you knew today's workout was your last, how would you treat it differently?
2. Do you have an appreciation for your coaches that you have never shared?

3. How will you ask the Lord to show you how you can be more loving toward your teammates?

Workout
Psalm 133:1; John 17:11,20; 1 Thessalonians 5:16-18

Overtime
Lord, forgive me for taking things for granted. I want to make today count. Please teach me to pray and help me demonstrate Your love for others. Amen.

Journal

6

Breaking Free

Ready

Now the Lord is the Spirit, and where the Spirit of
the Lord is, there is freedom.

2 CORINTHIANS 3:17

Set

In 2008, I made my first U.S. Olympic Soccer Team. I was still in college, and I was one of the youngest players on the roster. I was also replacing star player Abby Wambach who couldn't compete due to an injury.

Then in 2012, I was chosen for the Olympic squad again, but this time I was considered a veteran with several major matches under my belt, including the 2008 Olympic gold medal game and the 2010 FIFA World Cup. While both situations were very different, they were also very much the same. There was a great deal of pressure that came with the job.

The pressure of high expectations can be difficult to manage. If you have a bad game, you can't blame anyone but yourself. If you have a great game, you can be tempted to get prideful and unknowingly set yourself up to fall. The hardest part is playing free and not allowing the pressure to negatively impact your performance and steal your joy in the process.

In order to break free of the pressure that comes with expectations, there are some important steps that you must take. First of all, make sure that your confidence is in Christ—not in yourself. Secondly, understand that your identity is in Him. And finally, always keep in mind that your sport should be, as it says in Romans 12:1, your spiritual act of worship. Whatever talent Christ has blessed you with ultimately belongs to Him.

Those steps will help relieve the pressure from high expectations. They will also bring you true joy and allow you to give God the glory in everything you do. —*Lauren Cheney*

Go

1. Describe a time when you felt pressure as an athlete. How did it impact your performance?
2. Of the three steps listed, which ones have you applied to your life? Which ones are difficult to walk out?
3. Read 2 Corinthians 3:17. How might inviting His Spirit into your athletic life bring freedom and help you better deal with pressure?

Workout

John 8:32; Romans 12:1-2; 2 Timothy 1:7

Overtime

Lord, I want to break free from worldly expectations and the pressures that accompany it. Transform my way of thinking and fill my heart with the kind of joy that only You can bring. Amen.

Journal

7

No Excuses

Ready

But without exception they all began to make excuses.

LUKE 14:18

Set

When I was 12, I was playing second base for an all-star team. I still remember dropping that pop fly that ended up, in part, costing us the win. I made excuses—blaming the rain and even the lights (it was a night game). At the time, I didn't think I was making excuses; I just didn't want the loss to be my fault.

Excuses spread like a virus. We blame the refs, our teammates and even the weather! We make excuses for why we're late to practice, why we didn't work out, why we missed a shot—you name it. When we justify why we didn't do what we should've, it's easier to make excuses the next time.

"Excuses are the nails used to build a house of failure" (Don Wilder).

Every excuse we make may seem insignificant, but in the end it helps hold together a life of failure. Nobody sees the nails, but they are there.

In Luke 14, Jesus exposes excuses. Those who had been invited to the Great Banquet feast found many excuses for why they couldn't attend, but none of the reasons were genuine.

But they all alike began to make excuses. The first said, "I have just bought a field, and I must go see it. Please excuse me." Another said, "I have just bought five yoke of oxen, and I'm on my way to try them out. Please excuse me." Still another said, "I just got married, so I can't come" (Luke 14:18-20, NIV).

Excuses never make you better. And they don't change your circumstances: they solidify them. When excuses become a habit, we're running on a road to failure. These three words are a sure sign of an excuse: could've, would've and should've.

Instead of pointing the finger, we need to take responsibility and assume ownership of the problem. We must own both the problem and the solution. It's time to stop making excuses. *—Jimmy Page, Adapted from WisdomWalks Sports*

Go

1. Have you ever played the blame game? Why is this so destructive to a team?
2. Do you take personal responsibility, or do you make excuses? Why?

Workout

Luke 6:41-42; 18:9-14; Philippians 2:2-4

Overtime

Father, show me ways that I've become an excuse-maker. Help me to take personal responsibility and make changes necessary for excellence. Amen.

Journal

_____

_____

_____

_____

_____

_____

_____

_____

_____

_____

8

Play with Purpose

Ready

According to the grace given to us, we have
different gifts: If prophecy, use it according to the standard of
one's faith; if service, in service; if teaching, in teaching;
if exhorting, in exhortation; giving, with generosity; leading,
with diligence; showing mercy, with cheerfulness.

ROMANS 12:6-8

Set

I've been blessed to accomplish some amazing feats that only a handful of female basketball players have achieved. During my career, I've been honored to play on an NCAA National Championship team, a WNBA Championship team and an Olympic gold medal team. At Notre Dame, I hit the game-winning shot and was voted the 2001 Final Four's Most Outstanding Player. With the Detroit Shock, I was named the 2003 WNBA Finals MVP.

At the 2004 Olympics in Greece, however, I had a completely different experience. I was the twelfth and final player chosen for the U.S. Team. I knew going into the competition that I would not be a significant contributor, but I was nonetheless determined to prepare for whatever I was asked to do. Every day in practice I had the opportunity to guard Lisa Leslie, one of the best players in the world. And that was my role.

In Romans 12:6-8, the apostle Paul teaches us that we all have God-given gifts, and we are called to use those gifts for His purpose. This is true for all competitors, and it's true for all aspects of our life. As athletes, it might be the difference between leading the team and providing support from the bench. As Christians, it might be the difference between speaking publicly from a platform and serving others anonymously. But no matter what our role of responsibility might be, it's important that we remember to play with purpose, live our lives with humility and desire to make a difference through the love of Christ. —*Ruth Riley*

Go

1. What role do you currently play on your sports team? Are you satisfied with that role? Explain.
2. What do you think it means to "play with purpose"?
3. What can you start doing today that will allow you to embrace that principle?

Workout

John 15:16; 1 Corinthians 12:27-31; Colossians 3:23

Overtime

Lord, I want to play with purpose. I want to embrace my role and embrace the gifts and abilities with which You have blessed me. Help me transfer this principle beyond the field of competition and into every aspect of my life. Amen.

Journal

9

Influence with Integrity

Ready

The one who lives with integrity lives securely, but whoever
perverts his ways will be found out.

PROVERBS 10:9

Set

In today's world of sports, it seems that anything done for an advantage is fair game—as long as you don't get caught.

As a Major League pitcher, I have seen it all. Managers who
spend their entire careers stealing the signs of other coaches from
the dugouts and down the baselines. Players who reach base do the
same thing. Pitchers are supposed to throw a clean, unscratched
ball, but you can do some pretty cool things with a scuffed baseball.

As Christians, however, we are held to a higher standard. Our
goal should be to live a life that's pleasing to God and that allows us
to have influence on those around us. People seem to gravitate toward those who do things the right way. And on the other hand, if
you're not living with integrity, your influence will quickly be torn
down. If you're not trusted, then your relationships will have little
eternal significance.

In the book of Daniel, we read about a young man who lived
with great integrity. When he was given the chance to turn his back
on God's commands, Daniel stood strong and gained influence
over an entire kingdom. And, of course, there has been no greater
example of integrity than Jesus Christ. He was who He says He
was, and He lived a sinless life despite many opportunities to succumb to temptation.

Living with integrity in this day and age isn't easy. You might
say it's harder than ever before. But with God's Word and the Holy
Spirit guiding your steps, it is possible to be the person of integrity
that He created you to be. —*Adam Wainwright*

Go

1. What are some things that make it difficult to maintain integrity in today's world?
2. How would you define the relationship between integrity and influence?
3. What can you start doing today that will help set you on a path toward godly integrity?

Workout

Psalm 41:11-12; Proverbs 28:6; Daniel 1

Overtime

Lord, I want to walk upright in Your sight. Give me the determination to live with integrity through all that I say and do. Help me build trust within my relationships so that I might influence others for Your Kingdom.

Journal

10

Fundamentals for Success

Ready

Therefore, everyone who hears these words of
Mine and acts on them will be like a sensible man
who built his house on the rock.

MATTHEW 7:24

Set

The foundation for success in any sport relies primarily on the mastery of fundamentals. Champion athletes spend time perfecting their skills by focusing on fundamentals. At times it may seem trite, but to error fundamentally could produce devastating miscues! It doesn't matter at what level you compete, ignore the fundamentals and your performance will suffer.

Have you ever seen a wide receiver take his eyes off the ball and drop the pass even though it hit his hands? Have you witnessed an infielder looking foolish as a routine ground ball rolls through his legs and into the outfield all because he was more concerned with throwing out the hitter than securing the ball? Or what about a world champion sprinter standing straight up out of her starting blocks, anxious to win but forgetting the fundamental technique of staying low, and losing the race?

In the same manner, if we overlook the foundations of our Christian walk, the challenges of life could leave us humiliated. Reading the Word of God and conversing with our Lord through prayer are the one-two punch of Christian fundamentals. We must center our hearts and minds on the truths of God's Word and pray His promises over our lives daily.

These practices will aid in our decision making, our pursuits, our passion and our purpose. And when the rushing waters of life come our way, though He may not build a bridge, He will certainly stand with us so the waters will not overcome! —*Steve Fitzhugh*

Go

1. Can you remember a time in competition when you had a lapse in fundamentals and made an error? How did that make you feel?
2. Can you think of a talented athlete with tremendous potential who didn't have a foundation deep enough to sustain success?
3. What commitments have you made (or will you make) to master the two biblical foundations of prayer and reading God's Word?

Workout

Matthew 7:24-27; Luke 21:36; Acts 17:11

Overtime

Thank You, Lord, for Your purpose and will for my life. Give me the strength to commit to reading Your Word and talking with You daily. Allow Your presence to abide in me so I can take on any challenge that comes my way. Amen.

Journal

_____

_____

_____

_____

_____

_____

_____

_____

_____

_____

_____

_____

11

The Path of Freedom

Ready

Now the Lord is the Spirit, and where the Spirit
of the Lord is, there is freedom.

2 CORINTHIANS 3:17

Set

Los Angeles Angels All-Star Josh Hamilton's career was initially derailed by the abuse of and addiction to drugs and alcohol. After several stints in rehab, he was still unable to escape those vices under his own power.

Josh admits that at the time, he didn't realize how he was hurting those closest to him as his life revolved around satisfying his cravings for more. Once he hit bottom at his grandmother's home in 2005, his heart was opened to God's love and how much he needed Christ's help to overcome his addictions and heal the brokenness in his life.

Substance abuse can take on different forms, including drugs (illegal and performance-enhancing), alcohol, tobacco and numerous other things. But the answer to addictions and substance abuse of any kind can only be found by embracing the life and sacrifice of Jesus Christ. Paul encourages in 2 Corinthians 3:17 that through the powerful Spirit of the Lord we can receive the true freedom He desires for us.

Like Hamilton, we may not be able to overcome substance abuse and addiction under our strength, but with Christ as our focal point and the support of Christ-followers we can begin walking down the path to freedom and recovery. Just like the path of addiction, the road to recovery is long. But once we understand we can never overcome our sin-filled nature on our own and accept Christ's sacrificial gift of grace and forgiveness in our lives, we can experience freedom in every area of our lives. —*Clay Meyer*

Go

1. Are you allowing anything in your life to become all-consuming to the point of addiction? If so, what?
2. How has your relationship with Christ provided you freedom from sin?
3. If you are struggling with substance abuse or the like, who is a trusted friend or mentor with whom you can share your struggles? Commit to sharing with them today.

Workout

Psalm 73:23-26; Philippians 3:7-21; Hebrews 12:1-2

Overtime

Father in Heaven, even though I realize my life and everything in it is Yours, I oftentimes place other things at the center. I pray that through Your Son I can be loosened from the chains that are holding me back from receiving Your blessings. May all I have be Yours, and may I focus on You being the center of my life. Amen.

(If you are currently in the middle of an addiction of any kind, reach out to a trusted friend for help and accountability.)

Journal

_____
_____
_____
_____
_____
_____
_____
_____
_____
_____

12

Punting into the Wind

Ready
But let him ask in faith without doubting. For the doubter
is like the surging sea, driven and tossed by the wind.

JAMES 1:6

Set

As a coach, my faith was wavering. I watched my unpredictable punter
jog onto the field, doubt washed over me with every step. I never
knew what to expect. It might go 40 yards in a tight spiral, or it could
be a 10-yard shank off the side of his foot. Every kick was an unpredictable adventure.

It was late in the game and field position was critical as my team
lined up in punt formation. As the punter waited for the snap from
center, the unexpected happened. The gentle breeze that had been
blowing all night suddenly transformed into a stiff wind. My punter
handled the snap cleanly, took two steps and kicked the ball high
into the air.

At that point, the play seemed to move in slow motion. Everyone
watched as a gust of wind caught the ball in midflight and pushed it
backward! When the ball finally came to rest and the official blew his
whistle, we realized we had witnessed an unbelievable negative 10-
yard punt. My doubts had been confirmed and the untimely wind
had managed to make a bad situation worse.

Too often we approach God with the same doubt as I did my
punter. Sometimes we're optimistic and sometimes we're pessimistic.
We know God can do it, but the results don't always turn out like we
want. We know God cares about us and loves us, but why don't we always get a positive result?

When doubt creeps into our faith, we often get tossed around
and pushed backward like that wind-blown punt. Our doubt does
not honor God and chances are slim that wisdom and insight will

come from our wishy-washy belief. Want better results? Take a firm stand the next time you pray, talk to God with complete faith in His Word and remember, no doubting allowed! —*Charles Gee*

Go

1. Have there been times you doubted God?
2. How does doubt cripple your faith?
3. Why do you think that God doesn't give us everything we ask for?

Workout
Mark 4:35-41; Philippians 4:4-7

Overtime
Heavenly Father, protect me from the winds of doubt. Teach me to be strong in my faith and to trust You in all things. Amen.

Journal

_____

_____

_____

_____

_____

_____

_____

_____

_____

_____

_____

_____

_____

_____

_____

13

Play with Passion

Ready

Whatever you do, do it enthusiastically, as something
done for the Lord and not for men.

COLOSSIANS 3:23

Set

Throughout my WNBA career, I've been known as a highly competitive player. I use every inch or margin within the rules of the game to my advantage. It used to really bother me when I was accused of being a dirty player. I sought out wise counsel from people close to me like my husband and my mother. I also had some in-depth conversations with fellow believer and WNBA legend Lisa Leslie and our team chaplain.

I ultimately came to the conclusion that if I'm not being competitive then I'm not giving my best to God. So I had to figure how to maintain my edge without losing my godliness. It took me a few years before I got it down pat, but I finally came to understand how to push and fight with the best of them and never get to the point where it made me think, say or do ungodly things. Once I was able to put a harness on my passion, that's when I was truly able to glorify Him through basketball.

Playing with passion is all about giving God your best and striving for excellence. This goes beyond the court and into every aspect of my life. It's about me having a passion for serving others, being a good wife, telling others about the Lord and doing everything "enthusiastically" for Him.

As an athlete, it's important to let that passion show up when you train, practice and play your sport. But it's just as important to strive for the same level of excellence in your relationship with God, your relationship with others and anything that He calls you to do. That's living a life consumed with God's passion. —*DeLisha Milton-Jones*

Go

1. What are you most passionate about?
2. What do you think is the connection between passion and excellence?
3. Read Colossians 3:23. How can you strive for excellence in all areas of your life, not just the thing you are most passionate about?

Workout

Ecclesiastes 9:10; Matthew 5:14-16; 2 Timothy 4:7

Overtime

Lord, light a fire of passion within my heart so that I might strive for excellence in everything I do. I want to passionately pursue You, serve others and play my sport to Your glory. Amen.

Journal

14

Resist the Devil

Ready

Therefore, submit to God. But resist the Devil,
and he will flee from you.

JAMES 4:7

Set

There are many things in this life that can poison your heart. In college, it might be alcohol, drugs or toxic relationships. As a professional athlete, those temptations are often in the form of material possessions and money. But when I committed my life to Christ during my playing days at the University of Nebraska, I allowed Him to fill the void in my heart that worldly things could never satisfy. I was finally at peace.

No matter how long you have been serving the Lord, the enemy of your soul is going to tempt you to walk away from the straight and narrow path. Thankfully, when I began playing for the Buffalo Bills, I had a group of like-minded individuals to help me stay the course. I also became actively involved in Bible studies and grew in my knowledge of His Word.

Jesus set the perfect example of how to resist the things of this world. He surrounded Himself with a group of men who wanted to please God, and He studied God's Word daily. When He faced a difficult test in the wilderness (see Matthew 4:1-11), Jesus was able to stand firm against Satan's temptations, even though His body had been weakened by a 40-day fast.

When you face temptations within sport and life, remember that you don't have to carry those burdens by yourself. It's too much for any person to go through alone. Find other believers that will hold you accountable, stay consistent in your Bible devotion and then you will be able to fully "submit to God" and "resist the Devil."
—*Chris Kelsay*

Go

1. What are some temptations that you face as a competitor? What can you do to resist those temptations?
2. Why do you think it's important to surround yourself with faithful followers of Christ?
3. Read Matthew 4:1-11. What lessons can you apply to your life after reading how Jesus resisted Satan?

Workout

Psalm 119:11; Matthew 4:1-11; 26:41; 1 Corinthians 10:13

Overtime

Lord, give me the strength to resist the devil and say no to temptation. Put people in my life that will help me make right choices. Increase my desire to study Your Word so that I might not sin against You. Amen.

Journal

_____

_____

_____

_____

_____

_____

_____

_____

_____

_____

_____

_____

_____

_____

_____

_____

15

Where Is Your Focus?

Ready

Therefore, since we also have such a large cloud of
witnesses surrounding us, let us lay aside every weight and the
sin that so easily ensnares us. Let us run with endurance the
race that lies before us, keeping our eyes on Jesus.

HEBREWS 12:1-2

Set

The 2004 volleyball season was my toughest as a coach. The first month I dealt with gym floor repairs, having items stolen out of the girls' lockers, injuries, bus break downs, playing time complaints, the first losing season of my career—the list went on and on. I invested a great deal of time preparing and planning and this is not what I had envisioned for this team. It was during the time, though, that I found encouragement from Hebrews by remembering to look around, look down and look up.

Look Around—"Therefore, since we also have such a large cloud of witnesses surrounding us." Imagine standing at midcourt in an arena, where every seat is filled with God's people cheering you on. Look around, God is cheering. We are not alone.

Look Down—"Let us lay aside every weight and the sin that so easily ensnares us." I've never seen a track star leave her ankle weights or training gear on as she approaches the starting line. The athlete will strip off anything that causes their performance to slack. As a child of God, what is causing me to stumble? What is evident in my life that needs to change? Get rid of it!

Look Up—"Keeping our eyes on Jesus." From the day He entered this earth in a stable, to the day He was unfairly put on trial, beaten and crucified, Jesus gives us encouragement to live this life of faith. He is our mentor, the center of our focus. When we look at Jesus, we should be encouraged to endure.

Endure the race, endure the season, endure what is happening in your life by looking around, down and focusing on our Champion Jesus Christ! —*Rex Stump*

Go

1. How do you deal with frustration?
2. What things do you need to "lay aside"?
3. Is your focus solely on Jesus Christ? Why or why not?

Workout

James 1:12; 1 Peter 1:6

Overtime

Heavenly Father, thank You for cheering me on. Help me to stay focused on You as I run this race of faith. Amen.

Journal

_____

_____

_____

_____

_____

_____

_____

_____

_____

_____

_____

_____

_____

_____

16

Joy in Victory

Ready

LORD, the king finds joy in Your strength. How greatly he rejoices in Your victory! You have given him his heart's desire and have not denied the request of his lips.

PSALM 21:1-2

Set

Is there anything in sport that can match the joy of winning? Those feelings of excitement, fulfillment and satisfaction which are conspicuously absent in a loss. There is nothing quite like experiencing triumph over one's opponent. And King David, the writer of Psalms 21, was extremely familiar with these emotions as well. In reading verses 1-2, Who did David credit as being the source of his victories? It surely wasn't himself. He said, "Lord, the king finds joy in Your strength."

For the king and for us, the great joy in victories comes as a gift from God. Like David, we should rejoice in the strength we feel in sport, but not due to our own efforts. It is God that has granted us all the deep desires of our hearts; we're greatly blessed just to be competitors in sport. We must constantly remind ourselves that the joy we feel in victory is an extension of God's blessing and not of our own accomplishments.

As you pray in preparation for competition, seek for God to focus your heart on His strength. Compete in great freedom, knowing God's power is your provision. And be mindful that it's His joy that should be your source of fulfillment, not the final score. —*Roger Lipe*

Go

1. What are some of your favorite feelings which come with victory in competitive sports?
2. How and when do you sense the Lord's presence and pleasure with you as you compete?

3. How can you cultivate a sense of joy in your sporting experience?

Workout
Romans 12:1-2; Ephesians 2:10; Colossians 3:23

Overtime
Thank You, Father, for Your joy. I pray that I will point to You in victory, knowing You are the source of my strength and the ultimate fulfillment of my life. Amen.

Journal

17

Followership

Ready

For even the Son of Man did not come to be served,
but to serve, and to give his life—a ransom for many.

MARK 10:45

Set

NBA point guard Chauncey Billups said, "To be a good leader, at some point you have to be a good follower. I was always a good follower. I always followed the right people and listened to the right things. Those helped shape me as a leader." So, what about you? Are you a good follower?

I can't tell you how many times growing up I was asked, "Are you a leader or a follower?" I heard it from my youth pastor, parents, coaches and friends. A subtle principle was communicated through that question: be a leader not a follower!

However, if everyone is leading, then who is following? I've never heard athletes or coaches confess, "I'm just a follower. Leadership isn't for me." Especially in our recognition-driven society, we all want to lead. Volumes have been written on leadership, but very little on followership.

What society is missing is that followership is the beginning of leadership. The best competitors have mastered the art of following and that's why people are drawn to them. Following does not mean going with the flow and doing what everyone else is doing. Following means intentionally watching and learning from others. You observe those who are walking in a manner worthy of the Lord, who live with humility and courage, who exhibit integrity and compassion, who make wise decisions, and then you choose to follow in their footsteps.

You don't follow others based on championships, title or position but example and influence. As Paul urges us in 1 Corinthians 11: "Follow my example as I follow the example of Christ" (*NIV*). Followership

starts at the foot of the cross. We must be willing to pick up our cross and follow Him daily. Remember, when you follow well, you lead well.
—*Dan Britton, Adapted from WisdomWalks Sports*

Go

1. How can followership change your team, family, school, church and community?
2. Why is it hard to be a follower as an athlete?
3. Who do you know who is a great follower? What makes that person a great follower?

Workout
Luke 9:23-24

Overtime
Father God, I desire to lead before following. Teach me how to let go of my pride and be a good follower. In Jesus' name. Amen.

Journal

18

Game Face

Ready

The Lord God will help Me; therefore I have not
been humiliated; therefore I have set My face like flint,
and I know I will not be put to shame.

ISAIAH 50:7

Set

The lacrosse game was heading in the wrong direction fast. As a goalie, I was frustrated that our defense had allowed three quick goals in a short period of time. Our coach pulled me aside and said, "Wipe that look off your face! If your teammates see or think that you, as our leader, doubt for one second that we can't win this game, they will be discouraged and give up." It was obvious that I had lost my "game face."

Although circumstances, much like my lacrosse game, continually change, we need to have resolve like Isaiah and make our faces like flint or stone. Today, we wouldn't say get your flint face on, but rather get your game face on. As competitors, we know what it means to have a game face. However, do we know what it means to put on our game face when it comes to our spiritual lives?

As followers of Christ, our spiritual game face doesn't come from our own resolve, perseverance or tenacity. Instead, our game face comes from putting our trust in God, knowing that Christ has gained victory over our sin at the Resurrection (1 Corinthians 15:57). We don't know what tomorrow may bring, but as Christians, our countenance and demeanor should be unwavering, because we trust the promises of God's Word. Coaches and athletes, we are confident because our confidence lies in Christ, not in this world. —*Sean McNamara*

Go

1. Why is it so hard for us as competitors to place our confidence in Christ?

2. Who is a person in the Bible, on your team, or in your life who is flint-faced and determined in trusting God? What can you learn from that person?
3. What can you do today to move your confidence from yourself to Christ?

Workout
Romans 5:35; Revelation 12:11

Overtime
Lord, thank You that my hope in You transcends all circumstances. I desire to put on a spiritual game face all the time. I place my trust and confidence in Your character and in the promises of Your Word. Amen.

Journal

19

Trust in God

Ready

Trust in the LORD with all your heart, and do not rely on
your own understanding; think about Him in all your ways,
and He will guide you on the right paths.

PROVERBS 3:5-6

Set

As a professional athlete, God has entrusted me with a measure of
talent. That talent has allowed me to achieve a certain amount of success on the golf course. If I'm not vigilant against prideful thoughts,
it can be tempting to trust in my own ability. That's why one of the
greatest lessons I've learned in my life is dependence upon God.

There have been times in my life when I haven't trusted God
completely and I've done things on my own. I've trusted my thinking and my reasoning instead of living by Proverbs 3:5-6. When I
lean on my own understanding, it doesn't make sense to give when
finances are tight. When I trust in my own abilities, it might be easier to succumb to temptations on the golf course and hedge in areas of competitive integrity.

But when I put everything in God's hands, I'm telling Him that
I trust Him no matter what happens and no matter how bad things
might seem. It's that surrendered attitude of trust that allows me to
have the freedom and peace to compete at a high level. That's when
I'm able to play golf to His glory and let Him take care of the rest.
—*Jonathan Byrd*

Go

1. Within what areas of your life do you find it easy to
   trust God? What areas are more difficult?
2. Read Proverbs 3:5-6. Go through each of those commands ("trust in the Lord," "do not rely on your own

understanding," and "think about Him in all your ways").
How can you relate them to your daily life?

3. As a Christian competitor, what does having a "surrendered attitude of trust" look like? What can you do today
to put complete trust in God in every area of your life, no
matter what?

Workout

Deuteronomy 28:1-14; Matthew 6:19-24; Romans 8:28

Overtime

*Lord, help me trust you no matter the success or failure I might
experience. When I don't understand what's going on, give the
strength, the patience and the grace to follow the path that You have
laid before me. I trust You with every area of my life. Amen.*

Journal

20

The Squeeze

Ready

Now we have this treasure in clay jars, so that this
extraordinary power may be from God and not from us. We are
pressured in every way but not crushed; we are perplexed
but not in despair; we are persecuted but not abandoned;
we are struck down but not destroyed.

2 CORINTHIANS 4:7-9

Set

"If I had one word to describe you, it would be 'resilient.'" I didn't
know if what I was hearing was a compliment or not, but during
my weekly meeting with my college coach, she explained that I had
a resilient spirit. A few months prior, I had walked on to the team.
I had been put through "the squeeze," a series of fitness tests, athletic drills and competitions to see if I had what it takes to play at
the highest level.

Often as competitors, we feel "the squeeze" when it comes to
performance. Whether you're competing in a big game, coaching a
losing season or fighting through an injury, we all experience the
pressure of performing against outside influences or circumstances.
What grows us as competitors is pushing through and learning from
those "squeeze" situations.

Yet, as *Christian* competitors, we don't have to rely on our own
power to get us through "the squeeze." Rather, we have God's
strength and the life of Jesus Christ that empowers and sustains us.
Therefore, when we experience the pressure of maintaining a perfect
record or shooting a game-winning shot, we are not crushed. When
we grapple with a season-ending injury, we don't sit in despair. And
when we face harsh criticism or critique, we don't feel abandoned.
We find encouragement knowing we can tap into the extraordinary
power of God that enables us to be "resilient." —*Amy Elrod*

Go

1. Reflect on a time when you felt like you were in a "squeeze." How did you react?
2. What the word "resilient" means to you?
3. How can you show a godly, resilient spirit during tough times of competition?

Workout

Exodus 15:13; Psalm 46:1; Isaiah 40

Overtime

Father, thank you for being with me during my "squeeze" situations and sustaining my spirit. Give me the strength to focus on and reflect You, even when the competition is tough. Amen.

Journal

21

Fired Up

Ready

Consider it a great joy, my brothers, whenever you experience various trials, knowing that the testing of your faith produces endurance. But endurance must do its complete work, so that you may be mature and complete, lacking nothing.

JAMES 1:2-4

Set

Cut from the team. Lost the state title. Playing time disappears. Your mistake costs the team a win. As a competitor, all these things are considered tough trials. Add to that academic pressure or conflict at home and you can feel overwhelmed.

In Daniel 3, we read the account of how Shadrach, Meshach and Abednego faced one of the hottest trials in history. When they refused to bow down and worship a false god, they were literally thrown into the fiery furnace.

Adversity always brings opportunity. When they took their stand and fell into the fire, the soldiers who threw them in were killed instantly, but they were unharmed. When the king saw the unwavering faith and courage of these men and then witnessed this great miracle, he immediately recognized that "there is no other god who is able to deliver like this" (v. 29). When others see how we persevere and trust through trials, they believe.

Character is uncovered in crisis and formed in the fire. It will be *revealed and refined*. God forms our character the same way He forms diamonds—with time, pressure and heat. When the element carbon is forced to go deeper beneath the surface of the earth it encounters extreme temperatures and pressure. Those extreme conditions make diamonds. And when they rise again to the surface, they display the brilliance of the light.

God uses trials to make *us* unshakeable and *Him* unmistakable. The more *"heat and pressure"* we feel, the more *"heart and presence"* of

God we experience. When we face trials, we can do it with joy, knowing God uses pressure and pain to produce perseverance and maturity, which can be witnessed by others. Let your character be formed in the fire and see how lives are transformed. —*Jimmy Page, Adapted from WisdomWalks Sports*

Go

1. Have you experienced adversity that has tested your faith? If so, in what ways?
2. What is the purpose of suffering in this life?

Workout

Proverbs 17:17; 2 Corinthians 1:3-6; 1 Peter 4:12-16

Overtime

Father, I know that storms are not optional, but inevitable.
Let me rejoice when I face the "fire," knowing You are refining
me in the process. Amen.

Journal

22

Stay Focused

Ready

Forgetting what is behind and reaching forward to what
is ahead, I pursue as my goal the prize promised by God's
heavenly call in Christ Jesus.

PHILIPPIANS 3:13-14

Set

I want to be a better representative of God on the field. I want to play every down as a total release of the talents that God has given me. I want to give the same effort on the first play of the game when my body is fresh as I do on the 64th play when I'm dragging my feet and my body is telling me to give up. Accomplishing each of these goals requires constant prayer and focus throughout the game.

Jesus provided the perfect example of focus as He walked amongst men on this earth. He was single-minded about His mission and never let anything distract Him from fulfilling His calling. Even on the way to the cross, people spit on Him, whipped Him and mocked Him. Jesus could have brought angels down to save Him. He could have given up on His mission. But He was so focused on doing God's will that He refused to give in to His flesh.

As a Christian, my mission is to love God and love others, but it's impossible to stay focused on this purpose without an active relationship with God through daily prayer and devotion. In Philippians 3:13-14, the apostle Paul also teaches that we must forget the past and reach forward to "the prize" of eternal life. When things get tough—on the field or in life—looking toward that ultimate future can truly keep us focused on what's really important. —*Roy Helu Jr.*

Go

1. How would you describe your mission as a Christian competitor? What are some things that tend to distract you from accomplishing that mission?

2. Read Philippians 3:13-14. How might "forgetting what is behind" and "reaching forward to what is ahead" impact your focus?
3. What are some things that you can start doing today that will help you stay focused on your mission?

Workout
Psalm 119:15; Hebrews 12:1-2; James 1:2-4

Overtime
Lord, help me to stay focused on the mission to which You have called me. Keep me from any distractions that might take me off course. Give me the strength to reach forward and pursue the prize of eternal life while sharing the good news of Christ along the way.

Journal

23

Linemen Mentality

Ready

It must not be like that among you. On the contrary,
whoever wants to become great among you must be your servant,
and whoever wants to be first among you must be your slave;
just as the Son of Man did not come to be served, but to serve,
and to give His life—a ransom for many.

MATTHEW 20:26-28

Set

There is little mystery as to why the "lineman mentality" is such part of my DNA. A handwritten sign reflecting this philosophy flashed like neon every day I walked into my dad's office. It read, "Don't worry about the credit, just get the job done!" You just have to love linemen.

Coaches know that football games are won and lost in the trenches; yet to the average fan, linemen are just oversized guys that get in the way of the skilled guys. In my opinion, linemen are very intelligent. They are also tenacious, relentless and stubborn. With little visible reward or public recognition, they serve their team and get the job done.

A little of the "linemen mentality" would serve us well in our faith. Like Jesus' disciples as described in Matthew, we spend too much effort trying to be the greatest. How often are we like the receiver who, upon entering the end zone, thrusts the ball in the air and breaks into a touchdown celebration? *Look at me, look what I did for Jesus!* But Christ said things are different in His kingdom—greatness is defined not by accomplishments, but by service.

The life of Jesus can be surmised in two words: serve and give. A humble King was born in a manger and died on a cross for the world. Are we worried about looking good and receiving credit or just getting the job done? Are we tenacious, relentless and stubborn when it comes to serving and sharing our love of Jesus Christ with others or more concerned with being noticed? —*Charles Gee*

Go

1. Are you motivated by receiving credit or getting the job done? Why?
2. How would you define the word "servant"?
3. How can you be a leader and a servant on your team?

Workout

John 13:3-7; Colossians 3:23-24

Overtime

Jesus, this serving thing is hard. I struggle daily with the "me first" mentality. Help me to see the ways I can serve my team. I want to be consumed to serve. Amen.

Journal

_____
_____
_____
_____
_____
_____
_____
_____
_____
_____
_____
_____
_____
_____
_____
_____
_____
_____

24

Winning Decisions

Ready

As for me and my family, we will worship Yahweh.

JOSHUA 24:15

Set

It was my rookie year with the Houston Oilers, and we were playing the Dallas Cowboys at Texas Stadium. We were losing late in the game, and I caught three balls in a row, the last one for a touchdown to win the game. Looking back, I see that the catch itself wasn't the win. That was simply the result of all the "winning" decisions I had made to get to that point.

Growing up without a father, it would have been easy to make excuses. After tearing my ACL my senior year in high school, I could have felt sorry for myself. Attending a small Division II school, I could have given up on my NFL dream. Each moment provided a fork in the road, and I was going to have to live with the decisions I made.

Winning is all about your decisions. Notice there is a big "I" in the middle of win. For a team to be the best, you must be the best you can be. Winning isn't always about talent but, your commitment. There is a big "I" in the middle of commitment. Commitment is all about your attitude, and there is a big "I" in the middle of attitude. Attitude is all about your choice. By the way, there is a big "I" in the middle of choice too.

Joshua didn't say, "Let's all serve the Lord." He said, "As for me and my family." You can't choose for everyone but, you can and must decide for yourself.

It all starts with God's Word. His Word has the power to transform your thoughts, your actions and your circumstances. Never allow others to dictate your life, never allow your current situation to determine your future, and always trust God to accomplish the purposes that He has placed in your heart. —*Wade Hopkins*

Go

1. What are some decisions you've made during difficult circumstances?
2. How have the outcomes changed your life?
3. According to God's Word, how should you respond to challenging times?

Workout

1 Kings 18; 2 Kings 22; Colossians 1:16

Overtime

Father, I know you have a wonderful plan for my life.
Help me make wise decisions when facing struggles
and choose to trust Your Word. Amen.

Journal

25

What's at Your Center?

Ready

Jesus said to her, "I am the resurrection and the life.
The one who believes in Me, even if he dies, will live.
Everyone who lives and believes in Me will never die—ever.
Do you believe this?"

JOHN 11:25-26

Set

As athletes and coaches, we are motivated to think, "I can handle anything that comes my way!" We are trained to take on tough opponents and push ourselves beyond our limits. We are used to having challenges, but on my 52nd birthday I was faced with news that I couldn't handle. I was diagnosed with stage IV cancer and given six months to live. I was a surfer with an active lifestyle and no obvious health issues. The "C" word was the furthest thing from my mind, and the news was like a huge tsunami washing over my family.

In the days that followed, my family and I discovered that my diagnosis was taking its toll on us. The problem was that our focus was now cancer. Imagine the nucleolus of an atom, cancer was now the center, and we were revolving around an unknown entity that was trying to destroy us. We decided right then to pray and ask the Lord to be our center, that He and our family together would be the nucleus. With God's power we pushed cancer to the outer rim of the atom, making it seem smaller, having less influence on our lives. It was just something that we're dealing with through Christ's awesome strength.

Have you been living your life on your own strength, thinking you can handle it alone? Can you truly say you put your faith and trust in God more than your own abilities? Commit to surrendering every area of your life, including sports, to the strength of God. Let Him be your center and push everything—sports, life, success, challenges, sickness—to the outer rim. —*Joe Matera*

Go

1. What would you do if you found out today that you were terminally ill?
2. Is God at the center of your life? Why or why not?
3. What distractions need to be pushed into the "outer rim"?

Workout

Isaiah 41:18-20; John 11:4; Romans 5:2-5

Overtime

Lord Jesus, thank you for being my hope and strength.
Help me push aside anything that is distracting me from focusing
on your love and promises. Amen.

Journal

26

It's All Good

Ready

Noah was a righteous man, blameless among his
contemporaries; Noah walked with God.

GENESIS 6:9

Set

"Dad, it's all good! Everybody is doing it." This was exactly what my
oldest daughter told me when she decided it was okay to say, "I swear
to G–." Well, I don't really like that statement, and so I declared that
it wasn't "all good" in my house!

When we are faced with peer pressure, it ends up having some
kind of huge power over us. Our tendency is to buy-in and participate . . . whether it's good or bad. For example, when you are competing in a game where everybody seems to be a bit agitated and the bad
language and attitudes are flying, it might be easy for you to join in.

Noah lived in a day where everybody was joining in and doing it.
The Bible says, "Now the earth was corrupt in God's sight, and the
earth was filled with wickedness" (Genesis 6:11). It was so corrupt
that God decided to wipe everyone on the planet out! Everyone was
corrupt . . . except Noah.

So, how did Noah not succumb to the pressure? He walked with
God. A righteous lifestyle is not about fitting in. It's not about saying,
"It's ALL good." A righteous life includes purging the world and its
standards from your walk and embracing God and His standards in
your life.

Walking with God is a joy. It may be hard and seem odd at times,
but God rewards those that keep His ways (Psalm 25:10). So don't be
tempted to buy into the world's ways. Instead buy into God's. Walk
with Him daily, and keep your focus on what He says is "all good"
when making choices in life. —*Clay Elliott*

Go

1. What are some of the things that seem to be "all good" within competition but aren't godly?
2. Within athletics, what situations tempt you to "join in"?
3. What can you add/purge in your daily walk with God to reflect more of His righteousness?

Workout

Genesis 6; Exodus 15:26; Isaiah 5:21

Overtime

Father, I desire to hear You say "it's all good" as I walk with You on the field of competition. Give me the strength not to succumb to the pressures of this world. In Jesus' name I pray. Amen.

Journal

27

Form Follows Function

Ready

And whatever you do, in word or in deed, do
everything in the name of the Lord Jesus, giving thanks
to God the Father through Him.

COLOSSIANS 3:17

Set

The serve in volleyball is a crucial component of the game. The form of the serve, however, is not as important and varies from player to player. Some athletes dribble the ball three times before holding it out in front of themselves for the toss. Some skip the dribble but place their fingertips precisely over a logo or text on the ball's surface. And others step into a jump serve or leap from a standing position.

The form is different, but the function is the same: the ball's hit over the net. Frankly, a person's form doesn't really matter if the serve is effective.

In our lives, we serve the Lord in various forms. Some believers work in a professional ministry or a pastoral role. Other believers are college athletes, students, coaches, retail clerks, stay-at-home moms, teachers, etc. To put it bluntly, the form of our service to the Lord is not what matters. Form follows function. Our function as followers of Jesus Christ is to glorify God and serve Him with all our hearts. As Colossians reminds us, whatever we do, do it in His name. And no matter the form of your service, may you strive to ace the function of bringing glory to God. —*Christy Cabe*

Go

1. What does your service to the Lord look like in sport?
2. Are you bringing glory to God in all areas of your life, even in the small details?
3. Are you more concerned about what others think of your life or what pleases God?

Workout
Philippians 2:14-16; Colossians 2:6-7

Overtime
Lord, thank You for the opportunities to serve You. Help me to be faithful in the little details of my life, whatever they may be, so that I may bring glory and honor to Your name. Amen.

Journal

28

Eternal Focus

Ready

So we do not focus on what is seen, but on what is unseen.
For what is seen is temporary, but what is unseen is eternal.

2 CORINTHIANS 4:18

Set

Baseball has always been a way of life for Los Angeles Dodgers slugger Adrian Gonzalez. The three-time Gold Glove winner and four-time All-Star has excelled at the game since he first picked up a bat and ball as a young boy in San Diego.

But make no mistake, when asked to put his life and nine-year MLB career into perspective, he explains how his priorities have been, and always will be, about so much more than just the game. "No matter what—doing well, doing bad, statistics, box scores—all that stuff matters, but in the big picture it doesn't. I can't try to satisfy anybody here on earth, we're here to satisfy Jesus. You look at the big picture of life; there's going to be more time when it's going to be you and Jesus than in the field."

Gonzalez clearly has his priorities in order as a follower of Christ. He's more focused on his relationship with the Lord and sharing Christ's saving message than comparing stat lines and win-loss records.

So where do your priorities lie? Is your athletic career defined by how many points, hits, touchdowns and wins you can record? Or is the sole focus of your athletic career to bring God glory and lead others to Him through your success and defeat? —*Clay Meyer*

Go

1. Has your faith and foundation in Jesus ever been challenged by the desire to fit in with those around you? How did you respond to that challenge?
2. Does the desire to satisfy those around you cause pressure in your sport?

3. What does Gonzalez's quote, "there's going to be more time when it's going to be you and Jesus than in the field," mean to you? How does that impact your commitment to your sport and the Lord?

Workout
Psalm 27; 2 Corinthians 4:16-18; Colossians 3

Overtime
Gracious Heavenly Father, forgive me for the times that I pursue the praise of man through competition more than deflecting the honor and glory to You, who gave me the abilities you have. Let it always be my utmost priority to make your name known as I compete for You, an Audience of One. Amen.

Journal

29

Grace and Glory

Ready

But I count my life of no value to myself, so that I may
finish my course and the ministry I received from the Lord Jesus,
to testify to the gospel of God's grace.

ACTS 20:24

Set

As I recently watched a bodybuilding competition and saw the victories and defeats of the athletes, my thoughts went to the effect our relationship with Christ has on us as competitors. I think about my life as an athlete, the training I have endured, the elation at my victories and the devastation of my defeats, and I am reminded of the role God has played in this journey. Our lives are an absolute result of our relationship with Him and how we conduct ourselves as Christians as well as athletes.

I know now, after the years of competition, that it was God's grace that allowed me to stay healthy through it all. I also know that it is God's grace that covers me while I now train and compete as an over 50-year-old bodybuilder with multiple sclerosis. I am often asked how I can consider my life under the grace of God when I am afflicted by an incurable disease. How I can witness to the grace of God while going from a healthy athlete to one now battling to be able to train and challenged to even walk at times? My answer is that the grace of our Lord is not about our physical existence it's about the blood He has covered us with that allows us the gift of eternity in heaven. No matter how tough life on earth is, we as believers are blessed with God's grace. —*David Lyons*

Go

1. Do you see and feel God's grace in your life, win or lose?
2. Are you looking to Christ and His grace for strength when facing adversity? Why or why not?

3. Is grace a means for compromise or a reason for gratitude in your life?

Workout
Romans 5:17; Ephesians 1:7

Overtime
Thank you, Father, for Your constant grace and guidance in my life. Help my attitude, actions, and words reflect Your glory during competition. Amen.

Journal

30

Learning from the Best

Ready

Now if any of you lacks wisdom, he should ask God, who gives to all generously and without criticizing, and it will be given to him.

JAMES 1:5

Set

John Wooden, the legendary basketball coach who led UCLA to 10 NCAA National Championships, spent every off-season focused on learning a specific aspect of the game from those he considered to be the best in that area. He became the most successful collegiate coach by recognizing there was a lot he didn't know and that improvement could be gained by gleaning wisdom from experts in each facet of the game.

When the Bible speaks of wisdom, it is referring to God's perspective. James says that gaining God's perspective starts with recognizing that we need it. See the sarcasm in "if any of you lacks wisdom"? Clearly, we each lack wisdom. To gain wisdom, we must acknowledge that we don't have all the answers, that we don't even have all the questions. Regardless of our wins and losses, experience, giftedness or circumstances, God's perspective is best.

The great news is that when we realize our need for God's perspective on our game, our relationships, our circumstances and our lives, we simply need to ask. Not for God to fill our prescriptions for solving our problems, but for Him to show us how to receive more of His wisdom. We are not asked to jump through hoops or meet minimal requirements. God knows that when we see the gap between our lives and His will, the Holy Spirit will provide us with the wisdom needed for change. —*John Crosby*

Go

1. What is meant by not asking God to fill our prescriptions for solving our problems?

2. How can we "learn from the best" and gain God's perspective on wins, losses, injuries, important decisions, challenging people and difficult circumstances?
3. How do we ask God for His perspective?

Workout
1 Kings 3:5-14; Proverbs 1:7

Overtime
Lord, help me to recognize the gap between my limited perspective and Your perfect wisdom. Help me to see the records behind me, opportunities before me, people around me, circumstances surrounding me and thoughts within me as You see them. And give me the courage to align my life with Your will. Amen.

Journal

_____

_____

_____

_____

_____

_____

_____

_____

_____

_____

_____

_____

_____

_____

_____

_____

_____

31

Through God's Eyes

Ready

I will praise You because I have been remarkably and wonderfully made.

PSALM 139:14

Set

It might be hard to believe, but sometimes elite athletes struggle with self-image. I know this to be true because I have dealt with it myself. In 2006, two years removed from my first attempt at making the U.S. Olympic Diving team, I found myself fighting an eating disorder. I decided that enough was enough and that I needed freedom, so I attended a facility in Arizona to help me overcome my battle with bulimia.

You see, up until that point, I believed the lie that physical appearance determined my self-worth. When I looked into the mirror, I saw Brittany as the world did: a flawed individual whose value was based on external things that in reality weren't important.

But at Remuda Ranch in Arizona, I experienced real, honest and sincere relationships. I accepted Jesus into my heart and started a journey of self-discovery and true purpose with Him by my side. It wasn't easy. I fell back into my old struggles that next year at school, but had a teammate invest her time, wisdom and love into my life. Transformation took root. I began to experience light where there was once darkness.

When I look in the mirror today, I am able to see myself through God's eyes. I am reminded daily that He loved me even when I did not love myself. I am reminded that His forgiveness helped me to forgive myself and that His truth has replaced the many lies that had once overtaken my mind. And best yet, I am reminded that He sees me as fearfully and wonderfully made. I am His perfect creation—chosen, holy and dearly loved. —*Brittany Viola*

Go

1. Do you ever struggle with your self-image or with the way that others see you? Explain.
2. How can seeing yourself through God's eyes change how you compete?
3. Read Psalm 139:13-16. How might this passage help those with a poor self-image begin to see themselves as God sees them?

Workout

1 Samuel 16:7; Psalm 139:13-16; 1 Corinthians 3:16; Ephesians 2:10

Overtime

Lord, help me to see myself the way that You do. In those times when I don't feel worthy, remind me of the price You paid because of Your great love for me. Amen.

Journal

32

Seizing Opportunities

Ready
David said to Saul, "Don't let anyone be discouraged by him;
your servant will go and fight this Philistine!"
1 SAMUEL 17:32

Set
When I was recruiting, it was critical for me to judge if a potential player was a true competitor or not. True competitors are easy to spot. They are the guys and gals that are willing to do the things that most people shy away from. Teams and life are both filled with people that are willing to put on the uniform, but when faced with a challenge, they look for someone else to do the job.

According to 1 Samuel, David was a competitor. All he wanted was for Saul to give him the chance to fight Goliath. He wasn't fearful of a big challenge because he had prepared himself to seize the moment. He had already faced obstacles as a shepherd, defending his flock from lions and bears. This developed his confidence, making him eager to take on a God-defying giant. And like a true competitor, David knew where his strength came from.

When facing Goliath, he boldly told him that he came to fight in the name of the Lord. David knew Who was in control of his life and wasn't backing down from the opportunity to defend the name of his Lord.

Just like David, we have the opportunity to be true competitors both in our sport and in our relationship with Christ. We must continually prepare ourselves physically and spiritually to take on any obstacles we may face. It is the willingness to sacrifice and train ourselves to grab hold of opportunities that separates a true competitor from the rest of the crowd. Will you be ready to seize the opportunities God sets in front of you, or will you limit yourself to just wearing a jersey? —*Steve Keenum*

Go

1. What opportunities are you praying for God to give you?
2. How are you preparing yourself to be ready to face both spiritual and physical giants?
3. If presented with the chance, would you be ready to take a stand for God like David did? Why or why not?

Workout

1 Samuel 17; Revelation 3:20

Overtime

Lord, I ask for the opportunity to make a stand for You. I pray for the wisdom and strength to seize each moment you present to tell others about Your love and grace. Amen.

Journal

33

The Thankful Competitor

Ready

And whatever you do, in word or in deed,
do everything in the name of the Lord Jesus, giving thanks
to God the Father through Him.

COLOSSIANS 3:17

Set

A Christian competitor is a thankful competitor. Every time you step onto the field of competition, your heart is exploding with thankfulness, because you are abundantly grateful for God's blessings. You have a deep conviction that your athletic abilities have come from Him alone. Every stride, swing, shot, pass, goal and point is a response to God's goodness. The way you compete is marked with a "thank you God" because you count all of His blessings in your life.

You have been given much by the Lord, and you are simply grateful for the opportunity to compete. Your sweat is an offering of thanks to Him. There is no room for pride in a heart full of thankfulness. A thankful competitor is a humble competitor.

When you are thankful, you don't try to impress others. You don't care if you are starting when you are overwhelmed with gratitude to be part of a team. You don't put unrealistic expectations on your teammates' shoulders when you realize God's grace on your life. You don't care about the scoreboard when your definition of winning is becoming more like Jesus every time you compete.

You don't view competition as crushing your opponent when you desire to play in such a way that elevates all participants to a higher level of competition. You are not consumed with what others think, when you are focused on an Audience of One.

You don't criticize teammates when you believe the best about them. You don't have to play for others when you already feel God's pleasure. Be a thankful competitor! With a grateful heart, much can be accomplished. Let the power of thanksgiving change the way you compete. A Christian competitor is a thankful competitor. —*Dan Britton*

Go

1. What are you most grateful for? How do you show your gratitude?
2. How can you become a more thankful competitor?
3. When do you struggle to give thanks? When is it easy?

Workout

1 Corinthians 15:57; 2 Corinthians 9:10-11;
Colossians 3:15; 1 Timothy 1:12

Overtime

Father, I want to be a thankful competitor. Whatever I do or say, I will do it all in the name of the Lord Jesus, giving thanks to You. Amen.

Journal

34

Jump In

Ready

Therefore the disciple, the one Jesus loved, said to Peter,
"It is the Lord!" When Simon Peter heard that it was
the Lord, he tied his outer garment around him (for he was
stripped) and plunged into the sea.

JOHN 21:7

Set

There is a place in Africa where the world is split in two. A clear sign
marks where you have just crossed the equator. When you are to the
north of the equator the water moves clockwise down drains, when
you are to the south of the line, the water moves counter clockwise.
Whichever direction you start in, there is a gradual progression of
movement that slowly increases its momentum as you get further and
further away from the equator. And when you are standing on the
line, the water does not move at all.

The equator is a good illustration of our decisions for God. We
are in one of three places:

1. We are moving to the north of the line: progressing toward God's purposes in the right direction and on the
   right side;

2. We are moving to the south of the line: progressing grad-
   ually away from God's purposes to the left and in the
   wrong direction; or

3. We are stuck in the middle without any movement: slowly
   dying because of our lack of commitment.

You're either moving to the north or the south, progressively right
or dangerously left of God's presence. We are moving into a life of plenty
or constantly in a state of lack. You will either be like the disciple John

mentioned in verse 7 who recognized the Lord but did not move or you will be like Peter who threw caution to the wind and jumped in to be with the Lord.

Every coach wants an athlete they can depend on and who is committed. God is no different. He wants your consistency in love, faith and obedience on and off the field of play. Commit today to take the leap and jump in: into His plan, into His promise and into His loving arms. —*Fleceia Comeaux*

Go

1. How can you jump into what God wants to do on your team and at your school?
2. Are you moving progressively toward Him or constantly away from Him?
3. Is it time for you to make a decision and stop straddling the fence? Explain.

Workout
Mark 12:30; 1 Timothy 4:14-16

Overtime
Father, You are so loving and kind, so gracious and fair. Even when I do not consistently choose you, You are always choosing me. Help me to venture toward you with a willing heart and reckless abandonment. Help me to jump in with all I have. Amen.

Journal

_____

_____

_____

_____

_____

_____

_____

_____

35

A Bulldog's Nose

Ready

Therefore, since we have this ministry because we were shown mercy, we do not give up.

2 CORINTHIANS 4:1

Set

Winston Churchill once said, "The nose of the bulldog has been slanted backwards so that he can continue to breathe without letting go!" I'm not sure if this is true, but I love it. Think about that mean-looking, stubborn dog that has clamped onto an object and just won't let go! Talk about being persistent!

There is a story found in Luke 18 that encourages us to be persistent. Jesus tells us about a woman who was being treated unfairly. She persistently and repeatedly came to the judge asking for justice. Like a tough bulldog, she wouldn't let go!

It got to the point where she was driving the judge crazy with all of her requests. The story continues with the judge saying, "I will give her justice, so she doesn't wear me out by her persistent coming" (v. 5). Isn't it amazing that persistence gets the attention of others.

This is not just a story, but it is also a life principle that Jesus wants us to grasp and learn from. When you know that what you are holding onto is true and right, don't let go! Be persistent in your prayers. Be persistent in living for God. Be persistent in doing what is right and true. As a competitor, be persistent with your work ethic, with your dedication to your game and team, with how you respect your coaching staff, teammates and opponents.

And when you are persistent, you know it and so will everyone else. Having the ability to keep going is inspiring to others. Honor God by completing the tasks that He gives you with a determined, persistent resolve. —*Rex Stump*

Go

1. What causes peopole to give up and quit too early?
2. Has there been a time when you wouldn't let go? What was the outcome?
3. How can you be more persistent in your spiritual life? How about within sports?

Workout

Luke 18:1-7; 2 Corinthians 4:16-17

Overtime

Heavenly Father, give me strength to be persistent in living for You. I know what is true and right. Help me to take a bold stand for You each day. Amen.

Journal

36

Opportunity Through Scrutiny

Ready

For consider Him who endured such hostility from sinners
against Himself, so that you won't grow weary and lose heart.

HEBREWS 12:3

Set

Does crowd noise and constant scrutiny affect your athletic performance? Imagine competing in front of tens of thousands of screaming
fans who voice their immediate reactions to your every move. Add to
it the nearly year-round analysis by the New York media and you have
a pretty clear picture of what Yankees first baseman Mark Teixeira
deals with on a daily basis.

The bar has always been raised high for Teixeira, but it's something in which he thrives. "The attention means people care about the
game," he says. "That kind of pressure gets you pumped up and motivated to play a full season. I put pressure on myself, I want to be the
best player I can be every game."

And so it is with us as competitors. We must deal with the heavy
pressure applied by those around us—teammates, coaches, parents,
fans and so on. But do we thrive in the face of scrutiny, seeing the cri-
tiques of others as opportunities to excel? And on a deeper level, do
we also seize each moment of scrutiny to build up those closest to us,
pushing them forward while sharing Christ's light through love?

Consider the example of Christ presented in Hebrews 12. He
chose to pray for those who persecuted Him and endured insults and
ridicule far beyond anything we could ever imagine as He carried our
sin to the cross to pay the ultimate price and gain the greatest victory
in the history of mankind.

Let each piece of scrutiny you face be a new opportunity for excellence as you compete and coach for the Lord with everything you
have. —*Clay Meyer*

Go

1. What outside expectations and pressures do you face in your athletic or coaching career?
2. How can you handle those expectations more like Christ?
3. What opportunities do you see God presenting during times of criticism?

Workout

Psalm 40; Jeremiah 17:7; Ephesians 6:10-20

Overtime

Heavenly Father, we are constantly surrounded by people who each have their opinions on our performance and abilities. Please change our frame of mind to see those around us as people who need Your love. May we compete with boldness and excellence and, in turn, bring all glory and honor to You. Amen.

Journal

_____

_____

_____

_____

_____

_____

_____

_____

_____

_____

_____

_____

_____

_____

_____

_____

37

Seeking Treasures

Ready

Don't collect for yourselves treasures on earth, where
moth and rust destroy and where thieves break in and steal.
But collect for yourselves treasures in heaven, where neither moth
nor rust destroys, and where thieves don't break in and steal.
For where your treasure is, there your heart will be also. . . .
You cannot be slaves of God and of money.

MATTHEW 6:19-21,24

Set

Silence. All I could hear were the whispers of what sounded like disappointment from our coaches in the front of the bus and the sniffles of a few teammates behind me. Another loss. Another disappointment. We had lost so many games in a row at this point it was almost as if my whole life was falling apart. To the outsider, it seems utterly ridiculous to let a game control and consume your emotions, but to athletes and coaches, we know all too well the worry and anxiety that can overtake us.

In Matthew, Jesus commands us to store up for ourselves treasures in heaven, for where our treasures are found, there our hearts (and emotions) will be as well. If our treasure is our performance or the win-loss column, both of which will quickly fade, our priority and hearts are not focused on serving God.

When we allow ourselves to be so caught up in the things of this world, including sports, we lose sight of what's really important: our relationship with Christ. We cannot serve both God and the things of this world. We must seek Christ and His treasures first (v. 33). This will determine whether we will live in rest or restlessness. Anxiety and worry will not rule us if we choose to seek Him first and make our relationship with Jesus our coveted treasure. He is constant and He deserves our all. —*Amanda Tewksbury*

Go

1. Have you found yourself overwhelmed with worry or anxiety? How can you better surrender those emotions to God?
2. How do you define earthly treasures versus heavenly treasures?
3. How would your attitude or performance change if your focus was always on your relationship with Christ first and then your game?

Workout

Hebrews 13:8; James 4:6-7; 1 Peter 5:6-7

Overtime

Father, thank You that You are always in control.
Through Your Holy Spirit, give me a heart and mind that seeks
You and Your treasures first. Amen.

Journal

38

The Champion's Learning Curve

Ready

Now these things happened to them as examples,
and they were written as a warning to us, on whom the
ends of the ages have come.

1 CORINTHIANS 10:11

Set

The learning curve: it's a certainty within competitive sports. Champions have to be ready to learn quickly. There's not a lot of extra time during practice for excessive repetition. And sometimes, second- and third-string players get very little practice time and often no reps at all! Their learning comes through observation, and yet they must be ready to jump in the game at a moment's notice. And one of the biggest frustrations for coaches is to have an athlete enter a game only to make the same mistakes as the previous player.

True champions in life and sport learn how to succeed based on the accomplishments and failures of others. They use everyday examples to strengthen their resolve when facing the temptation to make bad decisions.

Judges 15 gives us a biblical example how some people just don't learn. One day, Samson took the jawbone of a donkey and killed 1,000 Philistines. What a sight to behold! One man versus 1,000 and 1,000 men die. When he stood atop the 990 dead men, do you ever wonder what the last 10 men were thinking? Perhaps they were whispering among themselves, "We can take him!" or, "He won't kill us, we are smarter than all the others!" Regardless, they died too.

I am sure we all know people who haven't learned from the bad decisions those around them have made regarding personal purity, drugs, alcohol and general disobedience. So why be like them and the last 10 Philistines. Why make the same mistakes as others thinking you can escape their regrettable fate? As champions, we have a greater learning curve. Let's be quick to learn from those around us and not hesitate to make wiser decisions. —*Steve Fitzhugh*

Go

1. What positive and/or negative examples in your life have shaped your decision-making?
2. Can you think of a mistake you've repeated? What did you learn from the experience?
3. How can you increase your learning curve?

Workout

Judges 15:14-17; 1 Corinthians 11:1; Hebrews 4:11

Overtime

Lord, forgive me for the times I've chosen to go my own way. Give me the courage to honor Your principles and gain wisdom from the examples you've laid before me. Amen.

Journal

39

Become a Cheerleader

Ready

For you have made me rejoice, LORD, by what You have done;
I will shout for joy because of the works of Your hands.

PSALM 92:4

Set

In 1936 the US Bureau of Reclamation and thousands of American workers completed an incredible man-made piece of work that cost $165 million dollars to construct. It was the Hoover Dam. The Hoover Dam is located on the border of Nevada and Arizona. It is 660 feet from end to end, 726 feet tall and took 4.5 million yards of concrete to complete. A major piece of work!

If you spend any time being a student of sport you will find some incredible athletic efforts that also took major work. For example, in 1954 Roger Bannister ran the first sub-four minute mile. Most experts thought this was impossible. Now, 50 years later many are running it 15 seconds faster than that.

Now, compare these kinds of work to God's. Take Creation; in the beginning God spoke the entire existence of all life in just six days! Galaxies, light, plants, creatures and his crowning achievement—man! And how about the virgin birth of Christ, a feat that had never happened prior or since. Talk about some awesome works!

Work by definition means to take effort. To compare the work of man in the Hoover Dam to God's efforts is a joke. There is no comparison, but somehow we marvel at these major earthly accomplishments while almost forgetting the unbelievable works God has completed. Can you imagine what it was like to create a ball of energy that sits in space 93 million miles from our own ball of dirt? This is incomparable!

So it should come as no surprise that when the author of Psalms 92 spent a few minutes reflecting on God's work, he cheers. I encourage you to do the same. Take time today to marvel at all of God's work and become His cheerleader! —*Clay Elliott*

Go

1. What earthly pieces of work amaze you? How do they point to God?
2. What other verses in the Bible celebrate God's work?
3. What work have you witnessed God do in your life that you can cheer about?

Workout

Genesis 1–2; Psalm 19

Overtime

Father, today I commit to be Your cheerleader. Thank You for the work You have done and continue to do within me! Amen.

Journal

40

Speak Up

Ready

But one of them, seeing that he was healed, returned and, with a loud voice, gave glory to God. He fell facedown at His feet, thanking Him. And he was a Samaritan.

LUKE 17:15-16

Set

After every practice and every game, Jessie would approach me before leaving the field and utter one small but powerful sentence: "Thank you, coach!" During the entire two years she played on our high school girls' lacrosse team, she never missed a single day of saying those three powerful words. Jessie understood the value of gratitude, and she wanted to make sure I knew that she did not take a single practice or game for granted.

Jessie was like the one leper in the story told in Luke 17 who returned and thanked Jesus. Out of the 10 lepers healed by Jesus, only one man scrambled back to say thanks. And notice he said it with a loud voice. He spoke up—loudly! I am sure that the other nine had an attitude of thanks but never applied their gratitude. The power of saying thanks is a simple thing, but hard to do. A friend of mine says that unexpressed gratitude can often be interpreted as being unthankful.

Thankfulness overflows if we have deep roots in Jesus Christ and if our lives are built on Him. Is it any wonder thankfulness is in short supply? As Christian competitors, if we are *over-full* with God, then we *overflow* with thankfulness. Otherwise, we are just selfish and stingy like many athletes and coaches.

No more withholding blessing and thankfulness from those that deserve it. What are you waiting for? Make sure you tell others how grateful you are for them. The power of thankfulness is in the action. Say it loudly! —*Dan Britton*

Go

1. Are you thankful? Would teammates, coaches and friends say you have a heart of thankfulness? Why or why not?
2. Who are three teammates or coaches you are thankful for? Why you are thankful for them?
3. What are the things that prevent you from expressing your thanks?

Workout

1 Chronicles 16:34; 1 Corinthians 1:4; 1 Thessalonians 5:16-18

Overtime

Lord, I desire to be someone who not only prays for those I am thankful for, but also who takes action and tells them. Help me to pray it and then say it. Fill me up so that I can overflow with thanksgiving. In the name of Jesus I pray. Amen.

Journal

41

Soul Food

Ready

Like newborn infants, desire the pure spiritual milk,
so that you may grow by it for your salvation.

1 PETER 2:2

Set

One of the most crucial moments in a newborn's life is the first act of taking in milk, their sole source of nutrition. Babies enter the world hungry and begin seeking the sustenance they were created to receive. Any newborn that does not desire to feed would be given immediate attention from the medical staff in order to help this function occur. Both the mother and doctors realize the nutrients milk provides are vital to the health of the baby.

When Nicodemus came to Jesus by night to secretly inquire how to go to heaven, Jesus plainly replied, "I assure you: Unless someone is born again, he cannot see the kingdom of God" (John 3:3). After we experience the supernatural rebirth of salvation, there is also a crucial moment that affects our spiritual wellbeing: desiring the pure milk of the Word of God.

Before being born again, our souls fed on the things of this world with hopes to satisfy. Always left malnourished, I searched for anything and anyone that would truly fulfill me. After hearing the gospel one night at a college FCA huddle, my eyes were opened to the truth and I came alive. Within the next few days, I noticed that I had a deep desire to know more about the One who saved me.

I wanted to know and do what pleased Jesus and I found myself, Bible in hand, feasting on the Bread of Life. As I consistently read God's Word I began to grow in my relationship with Him which also transformed how I lived. Not only does the Bible teach us, but it nourishes our spirit as God speaks into our hearts and minds. As born again children of God, let us not neglect the real "soul food." I pray we would seek God daily, meditating on the truth that endures forever. —*Alex Hagler*

Go

1. Why is consistency important in studying God's Word?
2. How can you incorporate reading God's Word in your daily life?
3. How can God's Word prepare you for competition?

Workout
Hebrews 4:12

Overtime
Father, help me to hunger for more knowledge of You and Your Word. Help me to consistently read Scripture and apply it to my life as a competitor. Amen.

Journal

42

Hand in Glove

Ready

Remain in Me, and I in you. Just as a branch is unable
to produce fruit by itself unless it remains on the vine,
so neither can you unless you remain in Me.

JOHN 15:4

Set

Do you remember your first baseball glove? Mine was a "genuine" Tony Taylor that I purchased when I was 8 years old. It was awesome! It rarely left my hand during the day, and each night I would rub it down with a generous application of saddle soap to soften the leather. To help shape the glove's pocket, I would put a baseball in the center and pull it tight with my Sunday belt. Then my glove and I would go to bed for the night. I knew this glove was going to make me a better player, and my confidence soared.

As time passed, I learned that the glove didn't hold any magical powers to help improve my game. The glove was only as good as the hand that went inside.

We can apply this principle to our Christian lives. My glove was a great glove, but its ability was limited. Without a masterful hand inside, the glove could not accomplish what it was designed to do.

If we think of ourselves as baseball gloves, our ability is limited without God's masterful hand working inside us. Jesus said that we can't accomplish anything unless we are connected to our heavenly Father. We may look productive on our own, but we have little hope of accomplishing our intended design unless we stay connected to Him.

The challenge is in our allowing God to constantly keep His hand in our lives. We must fully trust Him in every area. It's only then that our gifts and talents can fully be used according to His will. —*Charles Gee*

Go

1. Have you ever been challenged at staying connected with God? If so, what was (or is) impeding you?
2. Are there times when you trust things more than you trust God?
3. Why do you think it can be hard to fully rely on God?

Workout

John 3:16; Hebrews 11:1-3

Overtime

Heavenly Father, thank You for the simple lessons of life. Thank You for helping me understand that when I allow You to be the hand in my glove, You can use me to accomplish great things. Amen.

Journal

HEART OF A COMPETITOR

43

Never Quit

While He was together with them, He commanded them
not to leave Jerusalem, but to wait for the Father's promise. . . .
John baptized with water, but you will be baptized with
the Holy Spirit not many days from now.

ACTS 1:4-5

Set

If your motivation isn't greater than yourself, you will quit! Believe me, I've been there. As a current Master's competitor, there are times on the track when my legs are heavy and my lungs are burning and the first thought is, "go home, finish later." It seems that no matter how hard I work or how badly I want it, as soon as pain is involved or my commitment level is challenged, I waver.

It was the same for the disciples. The night Jesus was arrested they scattered like sheep. They had chosen to follow Him. They had left it all behind. They had experienced miracles and swore they'd never leave. They thought they were committed. But in reality, it was still all about them. When the chips were down, they didn't have the power within to rise to the occasion.

The same can be said of us. Whether as a coach or athlete, left to our own strength, we will give in and never realize our full potential. We need the power Jesus promised to provide in Acts 1 through His Holy Spirit.

Those same men who fled in fear became mighty men of God who died for the cause of Christ. What happened? What made the difference? Where did the ability to stand tall and courageous come from, even in the face of death? Through the power of the Holy Spirit.

So, whenever you face the temptation to flee from what you know God has called you to, dig into the power of His spirit and don't quit. —*Wade Hopkins*

Go

1. Have you ever quit something because it was too tough?
2. What things have you realized that you can't do alone?
3. In what areas do you need God's power?

Workout

Mark 14:43-52; Romans 8:11; Hebrews 12:2-3

Overtime

Father, I realize I often try to do things in my own strength.
I confess that I need Your powerful spirit living in me, giving me
the resolve to finish strong. Amen.

Journal

HEART OF A COMPETITOR

44

The Wrong Way

Ready

There is a way that seems right to a man,
but its end is the way to death.

PROVERBS 14:12

Set

The 2012 college football season kicked off with a great weekend of spectacular plays, exciting games and even your typical miscues. Unfortunately, Kent State's linebacker Andre Parker made the highlight reel for his blunder. Kent State punted the ball to their opponent, and during the punt a Towson player touched the ball, making it live.

Andre Parker quickly picked up the football and ran 58 yards, in the wrong direction. He was just 7 yards away from his own end zone, but got turned around and started running the other direction. Fortunately, some Towson players were just as confused and tackled him instead of allowing him to run into their end zone.

Life can present us with exciting moments: new job, new relationship, new season. In the midst of the excitement it is easy to get caught up and become confused! We get so excited about a new opportunity, thinking it seems right to us, we don't realize we're heading in the wrong direction.

In the Bible, Jesus tells the story of the Prodigal Son, a lesson in just how easy one can choose the wrong direction. There was a father with two sons. The youngest son acquired his inheritance early and with his newly obtained wealth, he lost sight of what really mattered. In his excitement, he became confused and morally went the wrong way. In time, the young man came to his senses, realized he was going in the wrong direction and turned around. He returned home, humbled himself before his loving father and found forgiveness.

Learn from history, before you make history. Become aware of the choices that lead away from God so that during times of confusion you, too, won't be tempted to go the wrong way. —*Rex Stump*

Go

1. What "ways" have seemed right to you, but led to pain in the end?
2. Do you know a friend or family member heading down a wrong path?
3. How can you help them find their way back?

Workout

John 14:6; James 1:5-8; 1 John 2:10-12

Overtime

Heavenly Father, sometimes I go in the wrong direction. Forgive me. Help me to follow Jesus Who is "the way!" Amen.

Journal

45

The Sweet Spot of Serving

Ready

Show family affection to one another with brotherly love.
Outdo one another in showing honor. Do not lack diligence;
be fervent in spirit; serve the Lord.

ROMANS 12:10-11

Set

We all have those games or matches in our athletic careers that stick
among the rest. Mine occurred during my teenage years. I was playing
at a national tennis tournament and had drawn a top seed. My opponent and I battled the purest match I've ever played before or since
with points won on effort, not errors. The number of spectators grew
with each game. Back and forth were the deuce-ads, neither of us willing to give up.

When it was over, I was elated. I had never played that well. She
and I hugged, drenched in perspiration. The score? 6-1, 6-1. (For her!)
According to the score I had been crushed. It was strange to feel simul-
taneously exhilarated and embarrassed. That score would be posted
on the giant tournament scoreboard for "the whole world" to see.

Yet, God taught me a valuable lesson on serving—not aces, not
others, but Him. As I was sheepishly standing near the scoreboard, a
coach and player saw the score exclaiming, "Who'd have guessed that!
It looked like a really close match." God showed me that while I
played, I respected her and her play (love and honor), and I intensely
fought for every point (with diligence and fervent in sprit). Because of
that, I served Him in that match. And on His scoreboard, I won.

In serving Him, I was in effect also serving my opponent, my
teammates and the spectators. And just like the exhilarating feel of
hitting the "sweet spot" for a blistering ace, perfectly disguised drop
shot or winning point, I had discovered the sweet spot of serving my
God. And no win could replace my elation. —*Nancy Hedrick*

Go

1. What is the sweet spot in your sport?
2. When have you lost in score but won in serving Christ?
3. How does serving Him in your sport serve your opponent, your team and the spectators?

Workout

Mark 12:28-31; Romans 12:9-18; Philippians 2:2-4

Overtime

Lord, even in the midst of competition when it can be the most difficult, help me to be in the sweet spot of serving; Serving You first by displaying love, honor, diligence and fervency in spirit.

Journal

46

Not Made to Draw Back

Ready

For you need endurance, so that after you have done
God's will, you may receive what was promised. . . . But My
righteous one will live by faith; and if he draws back, I have no
pleasure in him. But we are not those who draw back and
are destroyed, but those who have faith and obtain life.

HEBREWS 10:36,38-39

Set

It was the first game of my senior season at Appalachian State, and we were playing the University of Tennessee Chattanooga. Chattanooga jumped out to a 28-7 halftime lead. With 14:54 left in the game they still led 35-14. This game would prove our character and set the pace for our season. Miraculously, we came back to win 42-41. We did not quit or become discouraged by an early deficit. Instead, we fought until we achieved the victory for which we prepared.

Moments like this reveal what we are made of. They test our resolve. They test our endurance. Times of adversity and uncertainty are opportunities for us to endure in identity, discipline and purpose. When things seem to be working against us, in the middle of battle, we must be sure to stand firm in who we are, what our strategy is and what we are after. Identity means I know myself. Discipline means I play within my identity toward a greater purpose. Purpose shows me who is with me, who to stand with and what to believe in.

Endurance is the quality that separates the champions from the rest. As an athlete or coach who follows Christ, stand firm as someone who does not draw back, who endures and who obtains the promise.

Whatever happens in your course, do not stop until you see in reality the victory that God has placed in your heart. God is pleased by your endurance in identity, discipline and purpose. —*Blake Elder*

Go

1. What are the stressors in your life and on the field that tend to cause you to draw back from your commitments?
2. How can you resolve to stand firm in your identity, discipline and purpose in Christ?
3. What are some goals that you want to commit to achieve on and off the field?

Workout

2 Timothy 2:3-13; Hebrews 12:1-3, 7-11; James 1:2-4

Overtime

Lord, help me to keep my eyes fixed on victory like Jesus did when He endured the cross for the purpose set before Him. I pray I bring You pleasure in the way I compete and live by enduring to the finish. Amen.

Journal

47

Run to Win

Ready

Don't you know that the runners in a stadium all race,
but only one receives the prize? Run in such a way to win the
prize. Now everyone who competes exercises self-control in
everything. However, they do it to receive a crown that
will fade away, but we a crown that will never fade away.
Therefore I do not run like one who runs aimlessly or box
like one beating the air. Instead, I discipline my body
and bring it under strict control, so that after preaching to
others, I myself will not be disqualified.

1 CORINTHIANS 9:24-27

Set

There are a lot of people in this world that play sports or participate
in athletics, but not all of them are competitors. The difference? A
competitor plays with purpose. A competitor trains to win. A competitor plays to win. A competitor runs to win. A true competitor
doesn't just play to have fun, but with the ultimate goal being to win.

Paul understood the heart of a competitive athlete and knew that
as a Christian athlete we must train our hearts spiritually like we do
our bodies physically . . . with purpose. As followers of Jesus, our purpose in this life is to train our hearts to love like Jesus, to serve others
like Jesus, and to put our faith and hope in the Father like Jesus, in
every area of our life.

Jesus said it this way in John 10:10, "My purpose is to give them
a rich and satisfying life" (*NLT*). When we have Christ in our lives, we
are not just living but we have true life; life that is rich and satisfying,
life that has purpose and life that is running to win. —*Sarah Roberts*

Go

1. As an athlete, how do you train your body to win?
2. As a Christian, how do you train your heart to win?

3. What are three spiritual disciplines you can implement each day to train your heart to love more like Christ?

Workout
Romans 12:1-2; Colossians 3:23

Overtime
God, Thank You for loving me so much that you were willing to run your race with purpose, all the way to the cross. Help me to focus my life on the purposes you have set before me as an athlete and follower of You. Amen.

Journal

48

Grip It and Rip It

Ready

"Lord, if it's you," Peter answered him, "command me to come to
You on the water." "Come," He said. And climbing out of the boat,
Peter started walking on the water and came toward Jesus.

MATTHEW 14:28-29

Set

I love when people ask if I'm a golfer. I like playing golf, but I think
it's safer to say I'm an athlete who tries to play the sport. The best
round of golf I ever played came by following the advice of a friend
who can really play. He told me to play to my strengths and "grip it
and rip it": play with absolute freedom and confidence. I did, and it
worked!

When an athlete lacks confidence or is not willing to take risks,
they don't perform at their best. When you play not to lose, you lose.

I believe the Apostle Peter was the original "grip it and rip it" disciple; he was a spiritual risk-taker. Peter was the only one who took
the risk to walk on water. He eventually sank, but would never forget
what he was capable of when he obeyed the voice of God. Most people only remember Peter's failures, but Jesus saw his courage, passion,
energy and faith.

Peter wasn't a moral risk-taker, living close to sin or taking immoral
chances. Instead, he took risks that stretched his own faith and required
God to show up in miraculous ways. Peter was not afraid to fail.

As a result, Peter knew great victory but also humbling defeat. As
he took risks, Jesus refined him to be courageously bold. God took Peter's "risk taking" tendencies and put them under the control of the
Holy Spirit. We, too, can have a "grip it and rip it" spiritual mindset
and experience a life free from the fear of failure. When we boldly take
risks as God fills us, we'll begin to see the miraculous done in and
through us. —*Jimmy Page, Adapted from WisdomWalks Sports*

Go

1. Do you play or live with a fear of failure?
2. What are three spiritual risks that you can take to expand your faith?

Workout

Judges 6; Esther; Daniel 3; 6

Overtime

Father, take away my fear of failure and empower me to "grip it and rip it" in my spiritual life. Fill me with Your Spirit so I may walk with courage and boldness. Amen.

Journal

49

Turtle on a Fencepost

Ready

Let them give thanks to the LORD for His faithful love and His
wonderful works for all humanity. Let them exalt Him in the
assembly of the people and praise Him in the council of the elders.

PSALM 107:31-32

Set

There is very little in this world we accomplish on our own. I remember a very talented running back named Steve who was reminded of this principle during an afternoon practice. After scoring three touchdowns in the previous week's game, he was feeling more than a little cocky.

During a team scrimmage, Steve was coming down hard on the offensive line for poor blocking. Our line coach finally had enough and decided to teach Steve a valuable lesson. He told his linemen not to block at all on the next play, and he made sure to let the defensive players know the plan, too. You can guess the result—Steve got lit up like a Christmas tree! How easy it is to forget the contributions of other people in our lives. Like the old saying goes: "If you ever see a turtle on a fencepost, you can be certain that he did not get there by himself."

Take a minute to reflect on those who have helped you along the way. The list may include parents, spouses, coaches, teachers, church family and countless friends who have provided a helping hand when needed. These are the people that put you on the fencepost when you could not get there by yourself.

How easy it is for us to be like Steve and take all the credit for ourselves. Even worse, how easy it is to forget to give God a much deserved thank you. We call out for Him to do the impossible in our lives and when He delivers, we think we did it on our own. Take time to give thanks! —*Charles Gee*

Go

1. Who are some of the people who helped you along the way?
2. How will you take some time to personally thank these people for their help?
3. When was the last time you thanked God for His unending love?

Workout

Proverbs 3:5-6

Overtime

Lord, thank You for the influencers in my life, past and present. Keep me from taking false credit and teach me to always say thank you. Amen.

Journal

50

Living on Purpose

Ready

More than that, I also consider everything to be a loss in
view of the surpassing value of knowing Christ Jesus my Lord. . . .
My goal is to know Him and the power of His resurrection
and the fellowship of His sufferings.

PHILIPPIANS 3:8,10

Set

I will never forget my middle school coach, Coach Harris. Our team of
seventh- and eighth-grade girls would huddle eagerly around him,
eyes filled with excitement and readiness. What in the world could get
a group of easily distracted middle school girls so focused for a 3 PM
practice in the middle of the week? Purpose. Coach Harris consistently
filled our minds with goals and purpose for every practice and game.
We never lost a game that season, but most importantly, we never lost
the important purposes Coach Harris instilled in us.

Rick Warren in *The Purpose Driven Life* states, "Everyone's life is
driven by something." Warren explains that drive can be defined as "to
control, to guide and to direct." As athletes and coaches, we have endless
pressures of what should drive us: the desire to be approved by others,
wanting to be remembered, the hope of being perfect, etc. If we're not
careful, the purposes we focus on can be self-centered and temporal.

In Philippians 3, the apostle Paul looks to a more eternal purpose:
"to know Him." What if we competed and coached with the purpose
of growing in our knowledge of Jesus Christ and focused on leaving a
lasting impact through that relationship with Him?

Sport can be a limitless way to create a lasting legacy for Jesus
Christ if we live, coach and compete with His purposes. God has
given us all we need to live this life (2 Peter 1:3), but it's our choice to
walk with the purposes as He instructs. How will you choose to live?
—*Amanda Tewksbury*

Go

1. What drives you in athletics? In life?
2. Are there any purposes you feel God has specifically given to you for your team?
3. How can you better focus on those purposes?

Workout

Matthew 22:36-38; Ephesians 5:15-17;
Philippians 3:13-15; 2 Peter 1:3-11

Overtime

Lord, I know You created me for a life of significance: to love You and love others through You. Give me the grace to live this life focused on Your purposes. Amen.

Journal

51

Above Average

Ready

For we are His creation, created in Christ Jesus for good works.

EPHESIANS 2:10

Set

As a little boy, I had all kinds of heroes, including Hank Aaron, Walter Payton and Larry Bird. But not all my heroes were athletes. I also liked Luke Skywalker, James Bond and John Wayne. I didn't want to just be like the star athletes and receive applause; I wanted to make a difference by defeating the bad guy and saving the day. I didn't want to be average.

God created us each with special gifts and abilities. We were made to be above average and extraordinary—not for our glory, but to reflect our Creator God. The FCA Competitors Creed states: "I am a Competitor now and forever. I am made to strive, to strain, to stretch and to succeed in the arena of competition. I am a Christian Competitor and as such, I face my challenger with the face of Christ." That doesn't sound average or mediocre.

As a competitor for Christ, we understand that we have an opponent. In John 10:10 Jesus calls him (Satan) the "thief" who wants to steal, kill and destroy us. Our spiritual opponent has deceitfully rocked us to sleep, destroying our fervency by convincing us average is okay.

We need to wake up! We are competitors for Christ, created by a Holy God to do extraordinary things for His glory! We must commit to be a hero for God. And in order to defeat the "bad guy" we must be a spiritual threat. Mediocrity is our enemy's weapon of choice, and it's up to us to disarm him through the power Christ has given.

Psalms 8 says that God has taught children and infants to tell of His strength, silencing His enemies and all who oppose Him! God equips children and youth to be above average. And if God's done this for children, He's done it for us as well. Stand on that truth, knowing you were made for more than average —*Rex Stump*

Go
1. Who in your life inspires you to be better?
2. What are some threats to your spiritual fervency?
3. How can you be a bigger threat to your spiritual opponent?

Workout
Psalm 8; Matthew 20:24-28

Overtime
Heavenly Father, You created me to do great things for You! Revive my spirit and encourage me today to compete with greatness!

Journal

52

Identity Theft

Ready

Set your minds on what is above, not on what is
on the earth. For you have died, and your life is
hidden with the Messiah in God.

COLOSSIANS 3:2-3

Set

Each year millions of people become victims of identity theft. It is a
crime that leaves the victim feeling violated and a life totally dis-
rupted. Another epidemic is the loss of identity in Christ. One might
argue that it is also identity theft. That the enemy who comes to steal,
kill and destroy—the one who is the accuser of the brethren—is guilty
of identity theft in the lives of countless Christians.

Think of the thoughts, words and actions you had before you
had a relationship with Christ. Perhaps your identity as a competitor
was marked by anger, comparison or a performance-based value system. Now, your identity is in Christ. He loves you regardless of your
performance in sport or life. There is nothing so great you could do
to make Him love you more; there is nothing so awful you could do to
make Him love you less. He loves you that much! Yet, the enemy will
try to steal your identity in Christ, and the old habits of basing your
worth on your performance can sneak back into your life.

However, the loss of identity in Christ is more preventable than
financial identity theft. The key is reminding yourself of who you
truly are; who you are according to God, as He has described in His
Word. You are a saint, a new creation, Christ's friend and a light into
the world.

Start reminding Satan of these truths each time he tempts you
with thoughts of the past or false beliefs of yourself and your relationship with Christ. Know who you are in Christ and don't back down.
—*Kerry O'Neill*

Go

1. What does the Bible say about your new identity in Christ?
2. In what ways has the enemy attempted to steal your identity in Christ?
3. What is one Bible verse on which you can meditate to remember who you are in Christ?

Workout

John 1:12; Colossians 1:13; 1 Thessalonians 5:5

Overtime

Lord, help me remember who I am in You. Give me strength to fight off the temptation to think any less of myself than what is revealed in your Word. Amen.

Journal

53

God's Love

Ready

For Christ's love compels us.

2 CORINTHIANS 5:14

Set

As an athlete and a coach I have spent most of my life thinking God either loved me or was mad at me based upon wins or losses, good or bad performances, or injury or health. My view of God's love was purely performance based. Intellectually, I believed that God loved me unconditionally, but practically, my sense of self-worth and idea of God's love was dictated by wins and losses. When I lost or failed I went into the dumps thinking I was worth nothing and that God was punishing me for my sins. Repentance was motivated more out of the hope of receiving God's favor and a future win rather than true remorse.

There are numbers of athletes and coaches who are very successful because their entire identity is based upon their performance. This performance-based identity has driven them to levels way above the average because they have had to perform to feel validated or loved by God. Does this describe you?

Instead of our self-worth being based upon performance, performance should be based on God's unconditional love for us. We should compete because God made us to do so. With a heart of gratitude we should express the gifts He gave us. It is Christ's unconditional love and our relationship with Him as a child of God that gives us our true identity.

With an identity founded in Christ, our self-worth does not fluctuate based upon performance. Loses or subpar performances are not because God is punishing us. As His children, we always have His love and favor, not just when we win. God uses wins, losses and overall performance to draw us deeper into His love and plan for our lives. His love for us never changes! You are loved with an everlasting love and there is nothing you or anyone can do to change that. —*Al Schierbaum*

Go

1. Are you guilty of allowing performance to affect how you view yourself and God's love? Explain.
2. Why is self-worth is connected to performance?
3. Read Romans 8:31-39. What can you learn from this passage about God's love for you and being a competitor?

Workout

2 Corinthians 5:14-21; 1 John 4:7-21

Overtime

Lord Jesus, may You cleanse me of a performance-based mentality and help me to be secure in Your love alone.

Journal

54

Fighting for God

Ready

And this whole assembly will know that it is not by
sword or by spear that the LORD saves, for the battle is
the LORD's. He will hand you over to us.

1 SAMUEL 17:47

Set

Day in and day out Goliath stood on a hill across from the army of
God, taunting them to fight. Day after day they refused, fearful of the
outcome. For 40 days Goliath mocked, challenged and made fun of
the Israelites. And every time he came to the battle line God's army
would cower and flee with terror back to their camp.

But then one day, a shepherd boy named David came to visit his
brothers at the camp. After listening to the soldiers talk about the giant and hearing Goliath mocking God, David volunteered to fight
the giant and get rid of Israel's disgrace. He knew from prior experience that God would be with him.

David did not prepare for battle to simply beat his opponent, but
for the honor and glory of the one true God. He did not focus on what
his opponent was saying, but rather on what His God could do. And
out of a *pure motive came a pure victory*. He ran to meet the giant at the
battle line. With the power of God in Him and the army of the Lord
behind him, he defeated the giant with ease. Not because of his own
strength, but because he believed. He believed that God could do anything in him and through him.

Likewise, we must believe the same as David. We must prepare for
competition for the honor of God. We must focus on God's power
within us, not what our opponents might be saying. With God on our
side, we can compete with confidence, knowing His glory will be revealed, regardless of the outcome. And just like David, we must believe
that God can do anything in and through us as well! —*Fleceia Comeaux*

Go

1. Do you honor God when you encounter confrontational situations? Why or why not?
2. Have you ever found yourself in an impossible situation like David? Did you step up to encourage your team and lead the charge?
3. What can you learn from David's example that can help you and your team?

Workout
1 Samuel 17

Overtime

God, help me to remember that it is not about my strength but about Your Power in me. Encourage me to give my all when facing seemingly impossible situations but to recognize that You determine the outcome. In Jesus' name. Amen.

Journal

55

Overcoming Fear

Ready

The LORD is my light and my salvation—
whom should I fear? The LORD is the stronghold of
my life—of whom should I be afraid?

PSALM 27:1

Set

Have you ever faced someone who was obviously bigger, faster, stronger and more experienced than you? When this happens, another even greater obstacle often arises—fear. When we are intimidated, we seldom perform our best. Fear causes us to make mistakes. Fear blinds us to opportunities. Fear can cause momentary paralysis. Fear disables our reasoning.

"*Fear not*" is the most common command in Scripture. The Bible speaks more often of fear than compassion, joy or serving. God is concerned about our fear because fear is ultimately a trust issue. God calls us, above all else, to trust him. Fear and pride are the two greatest obstacles to trusting God. They are each about misplaced trust. Fear is about trusting in whatever or whoever you fear. When we are afraid, we put our trust in the ability or power of the source of our fear. Fear and pride reveal the areas of our life where we trust God the least.

We worship the God who spoke the world into existence, parted the Red Sea, gave David the victory over Goliath, raised a valley of dry bones into a formidable army, gave sight to the blind, healed the crippled, raised the dead and walked out of the grave. He is hardly challenged by our circumstances.

In overcoming fear, we must move our trust from the object of our intimidation to God. And to do this, we need to spend time getting to know Him and His Word better. God is completely trustworthy. And if you know Him, you will trust Him. —*John Crosby*

Go

1. Recall a situation when you were filled with fear, and then recall a situation when you completely trusted God. What were some of the similarities between the two situations? What were some of the differences?
2. What areas of your life reveal the most fear and anxiety? How might spending time with God relieve these fears?
3. How can you spend more time with God?

Workout

Psalm 46:1-3; Isaiah 41:10; 1 John 4:18

Overtime

Lord, give me desire to overcome fear by knowing You better. Help me to spend the time in Your Word and prayer needed to fully trust You regardless of my circumstances. In Your name. Amen.

Journal

_____
_____
_____
_____
_____
_____
_____
_____
_____
_____
_____
_____
_____
_____
_____

56

Soul Nutrition

Ready

God, You are my God; I eagerly seek You.
I thirst for You; my body faints for You
in a land that is dry, desolate, and without water.

PSALM 63:1

Set

This year is our year. A common phrase heard in the sports world. Hard work, hours of training and studying to hopefully achieve perfection. Eating the right foods to sustain a high level of performance on the field. Lifting weights to increase strength. Getting enough sleep. All in the hopes of having the best year yet.

As competitors, our lives are marked by a voraciously competitive spirit. We want to be the best athlete, the winningest coach or part of the perfect team. We discipline our minds and bodies to attain the highest level of performance, all in an effort to feed this insatiable appetite for competition.

As believers, we should carry this same deep desire to satisfy our competitive cravings into nourishing our souls. We hunger and thirst for a "win," but what about our relationship with Jesus Christ? Are we focusing our spiritual man to naturally hunger and thirst after the Lord. In our soul training, do we allow ourselves to snack on God-substitutes or use anything other than Jesus as our primary source of meaning, self-worth, comfort or fulfillment? Do we eagerly seek Him daily?

Author and theologian C. S. Lewis said, "We are far too easily pleased." As competitors, we wouldn't eat a diet of unhealthy foods and expect to perform at the highest level. So, in nourishing our souls, let us not be "easily pleased." Let's satisfy our hunger with the richest of foods—the Word of God. Let's begin devoting ourselves to devour the truths of God and acquiring a deepening desire where our soul thirsts and body faints for the Lord. —*Amy Elrod*

Go

1. What efforts do you make to secure a competitive edge?
2. Are there any "God-substitutes" in your life?
3. Have you noticed your soul hungering and thirsting after God? How can you cultivate that even further?

Workout

Psalms 42:1; 63; Jeremiah 15:16

Overtime

Heavenly Father, give me the same focus and devotion to You and Your will as I have toward my sport. Help me to nourish my soul with Your truths so my soul will continually hunger for more of You. Amen.

Journal

_____

_____

_____

_____

_____

_____

_____

_____

_____

_____

_____

_____

_____

_____

_____

57

Replacement Refs

Ready

Do not have other gods besides Me.

EXODUS 20:3

Set

During the first weeks of the 2012 NFL season, the use of replacement referees was the hot topic of discussion. Unfortunately, it wasn't for positive reasons. The replacement referees, chosen by the league because of an ongoing labor dispute with officials, delivered multiple ineffective performances.

The unimpressive and inconsistent management of the rules of the game became more obvious as the weeks continued. It was almost as if the players and coaches were treating these referees like substitute teachers—doing all they could to get away with infractions and even intimidate the referees to make calls.

In a similar thought, it seems that our nation is suffering from chaos and infractions because we have chosen replacement gods to keep order in our lives. Instead of living in obedience to God, Who gives us life, direction and purpose, we choose the replacement god of self-sufficiency.

Instead of making sacrifices to serve under the order of our Mighty King, we cheapen our choices for the gods of convenience and comfort. There are no worthy replacements for our Lord. It is He alone that provides us the guidance needed for life. Like a referee, God tosses spiritual flags to help correct our behavior and keep order.

In the end, without God "officiating" our lives, we are left with disappointment and disruption. And just as there is a cost to pay a professional referee to be on the field and bring order, there is also a price to having God in our lives. We must resist the temptation to use the replacement gods of the world and keep focused on God's instructions for our lives. Only then will we experience true peace and order. —*Rex Stump*

Go

1. Is there chaos and disruption in your life?
2. Have you given in to a replacement god?
3. Who will hold you accountable to make sure God is number one in your life?

Workout

Exodus 20:5; 34:14; Deuteronomy 28:14

Overtime

Heavenly Father, forgive me if I have replaced Your authority for convenience. Today I proclaim You are the only God in my life and I will serve You alone. Amen.

Journal

58

Vision Eyes

Ready
Indeed, the Lord GOD does nothing without revealing
His counsel to His servants the prophets.

AMOS 3:7

Set

At age 2, Craig MacFarlane was blinded in a tragic accident, but he turned his defeat into victory by becoming a world-class athlete who won over 100 gold medals in sports like wrestling, track and field and downhill skiing. He has even shot a 91 in golf! Craig doesn't have his eyesight, but he does have a powerful inner vision that fuels his drive to overcome. As a result, he has motivated millions with his vision!

It has been said, "One person with vision in their eyes can multiply and change the world!" Since the beginning of time, athletes and coaches who have vision in their eyes have shaped and changed history. There was a vision that was birthed deep in their soul and it changed the way they lived . . . and the way others lived too. They have vision eyes.

Every vision needs to have three key ingredients. If you have a God vision, not just a good vision, then answer these three questions:

1. *Is your vision too small?* If your vision doesn't terrify you, then it is too small. A God vision should be so huge, that you are bound to fail unless God steps in. You must get the "no way!" response when you share your vision. How big is your vision? The first ingredient of a God vision is terror.

2. *Is your vision too narrow?* If your vision doesn't include others, then it is too narrow. Having a vision doesn't mean you against the world. A God vision has to include others. God will rise up a multitude to embrace and own your vision. The second ingredient of a God vision is others.

3. *Is your vision just a daydream?* If your vision doesn't get accomplished, then it is just a daydream. Too many talk about what they are going to do and never produce any results. A God vision always gets done. It's not just talk. Take one step toward accomplishing the vision that God has birthed in your heart. The third ingredient of a God vision is accomplishment.

Don't let the pace of life, negative thinking or even doubts and fears kill your vision. Athletes and coaches, do whatever it takes to hear from God over the noise of life and pursue the vision He's planted in your soul. One person with vision in their eyes can multiply and change the world! *—Dan Britton*

Go
1. Is your vision too small? Does it terrify you?
2. Is your vision too narrow? Are there others who are part of your vision?
3. Is your vision just a daydream? Have you been able to start what you have been longing to do?

Workout
Proverbs 29:18; Habakkuk 2: 3

Overtime
Father, give me a vision so big that I am bound to fail unless you step in. Use me to impact the world. In Jesus' name. Amen.

Journal

_____

_____

_____

_____

_____

59

My Father's Eyes

Ready

For the word of God is living and effective and sharper than any double-edged sword, penetrating as far as the separation of soul and spirit, joints and marrow. It is able to judge the ideas and thoughts of the heart.

HEBREWS 4:12

Set

As a high school freshman, I was chosen to play on the girls' junior varsity team. This was a big honor, as most ninth graders played on the freshman squad. One week, the JV team did not have a game, and so I was bumped down to play with my fellow freshmen. At least "bumped down" was how I viewed it. I was arrogant and felt disappointed to be forced to play on what I deemed as a "lesser" team.

During a time out, our coach called us into a huddle. I am embarrassed to admit it, but I stood there, water bottle in hand, a few feet away from the huddle thinking I did not need to hear the coach's instructions. As soon as I tipped my head back to take a drink, my eyes drifted into the stands and met those of my father. That's all it took. Though he didn't say a word, the look in my dad's eyes spoke volumes to my heart. I immediately recognized that I had had a prideful and selfish attitude. Thankfully I was able to adjust my perspective and learn a valuable lesson courtside that evening.

Hebrews 4:12 tells us that God's Word has that same penetrating and convicting power as my father's eyes did during that evening. Sometimes we fall into sinful attitudes and actions, and we need our heavenly Father to help us get back on the track to righteousness. By fixing our eyes on God's Word, we can constantly adjust our hearts and lives in a way that is pleasing in His eyes. —*Christy Cabe*

Go

1. How often do you spend time reading God's Word?
2. Have you ever read the Bible and felt "God's eyes" meet yours and convict your heart?
3. Are there sinful attitudes or actions in your life that you need His help adjusting?

Workout

Psalms 25:4-5; 51:10

Overtime

Lord, I admit my pride, my selfish attitudes and sinful actions. Forgive me and help me to honor You with my life. Teach me from Your Word, Father, that I may learn to please You. Amen.

Journal

60

Quiet Gives Birth to Momentum

Ready

So Jotham strengthened himself because he did not
waver in obeying the LORD his God.

2 CHRONICLES 27:6

Set

It's the last at-bat of the 2003 American League Division Series. Red
Sox outfielder Trot Nixon steps up to the plate with millions watching
around the world. If he fails to get on base, the season's over for him,
his teammates, coaches and the entire Red Sox Nation. Nixon takes a
deep breath and prays, not to win but that God would calm his nerves.

He stays calm, looks for a pitch to hammer and hits one of the
biggest walk-off homeruns in Red Sox history, setting off a mob
scene at Fenway Park. In the midst of chaos and pressure, Nixon was
quiet. What a wonderful example of an athlete "ordering his ways before the Lord."

Dan Webster in his *Leadership of the Heart* series says that quiet
gives birth to momentum. Just like Nixon at the plate, we, too, should
pray for our spirits to be calmed. Through this quietness, we experience both God's presence and His guidance. And the momentum produced will keep us focused and lead us in the right direction.

Jesus sets the ultimate example of the need to experience quiet
moments with God in times of pressure. In Luke 6, He went away before making the important decision of choosing the disciples. In Matthew 14 we see Jesus separating himself from others after the tragedy
of John the Baptist's beheading. Maybe the best example is in Luke
22, when Jesus prayed in the garden before the crucifixion. It was here
He experienced the Father's presence and gained momentum to fulfill His purpose on the cross.

In the quietness of your heart, be reminded that God the Father is
available to you today. Whether you are facing a game- or life-changing

situation, God is able to provide you with the peace and momentum needed to fulfill His callings in your life. —*Scott Ashton*

Go

1. Have you ever experienced a time in your sport when you needed God to calm your spirit?
2. In what areas of life do you need quietness with God to help fulfill His callings?

Workout

Matthew 14:1-13; Mark 1:35-37; Luke 6:12-17

Overtime

Lord, I ask for You to calm my spirit today. Help me to seek Your Spirit for direction and the momentum needed to complete all You've called me to. Amen.

Journal

61

Every Day Principle

Ready

Very early in the morning, while it was still dark, He
got up, went out, and made His way to a deserted place.
And He was praying there.

MARK 1:35

Set

As an athlete, I always looked forward to the off-season. I was no
longer confined to the limitations of our team's program. During the
off-season, I could customize my training to improve my skills and
make the most of the opportunities God presented to me as an athlete. I thoroughly enjoyed the chance to elevate my game to a level I
had never experienced.

Every competitor would like to experience similar growth in the
off-season, but for some, the discipline, focus and desire is lacking. As
a result, they get out of shape when their season is over. To excel in
sports, athletes and coaches understand the "Every Day Principle."
Every day, I need to discipline myself in every area (spiritually, mentally and physically) to compete at my best. Not every once in a while,
but every day!

The Christian life can be viewed in a very similar manner. To experience all that is promised in God's Word, we must realize the im-
portance of being in prayer and strengthening our understanding of
God's Word and character every day. The more I trust God in my life,
the more fulfillment I experience and the more I desire to live a life of
gratitude for who God is and for all the many ways He blesses me.

As an athlete, you cannot see change or growth in your skills over-
night and the same goes for your spiritual life. To see growth in your
faith, you have to intentionally carve out time every day to allow
God's Spirit to transform your life. Jesus modeled this daily, as He
would continually withdraw to be in God's presence. You cannot

grow in your faith and take your walk with Christ to another level without daily worship. Start today! Make it a priority every day to discipline yourself and engage with God! —*Sean McNamara*

Go

1. How does your relationship with God today compare to the greatest season in your walk with Christ?
2. Is your relationship with God flourishing or withering?
3. Do you have a time and a place set aside for daily fellowship with God?

Workout

Philippians 1:5-7; Revelation 3:20

Overtime

Lord, thank You for the power of prayer. Give me the desire and discipline to fellowship with You daily. Amen.

Journal

_____

_____

_____

_____

_____

_____

_____

_____

_____

_____

_____

_____

_____

_____

62

Perfectly Imperfect

Ready

Be perfect, therefore, as your heavenly Father is perfect.

MATTHEW 5:48

Set

I need to coach this team to a winning season or I will lose my job. If I don't play him, his dad will yell at me. If I miss this field goal, game over. I need at least 10 points tonight or coach will be mad. There is a scout coming, I need to play my best today.

Expectations. Every coach and athlete has them. If you fail, circumstantial consequences exist alongside discouragement, feeling like a failure and the temptation to give up. What is often the result of trying to perfectly meet all expectations? Worry, fear, stress, pressure, etc. We think, *"I need to earn my place,"* or *"I need good results to feel good about myself and for others to accept me."* And, no matter how hard we try, we still fall short somewhere along the way.

Jesus tells us to be perfect as our heavenly Father is perfect. Hmm . . . have we met that expectation? Absolutely not! We have all fallen short (Romans 3:23). Yet, nothing we do can earn the love and grace God has for us. God shows His love in that while we were still sinners, Christ died for us (Romans 5:8). Because of our imperfections (sins), our consequence is hell, yet because of Christ's death and resurrection, hell can be erased from our destiny.

We will continue to fall short with God and man. But rather than letting the outcomes of your pursuits drive your perspective and attitude, live constantly from God's truth of Who He is and who you are in Him, trusting that His plans are best.

Strive to meet the expectations upon you faithfully and obediently, but within God's grace. This releases the pressure to be perfect (fear of failure) and gives you motivation to keep going when you do mess up. Embrace the grace, you are perfectly imperfect. —*Kristina Krogstad*

Go

1. What expectations are placed on you?
2. Do you live in fear of always trying to be perfect in meeting those expectations?
3. Study in depth the last paragraph in the reading in light of the Scriptures listed below. How does God's grace release the pressure on you to be perfect?

Workout

John 8:31-32; 2 Corinthians 12:7-10;
Philippians 3:7-16; Hebrews 4:15-16

Overtime

Father, help me live out of Your love for me rather than fear of trying to earn the approval of You and men. Amen.

Journal

63

Step Up

Ready

For it is God who is working in you, enabling you both to desire and to work out His good purpose.

PHILIPPIANS 2:13

Set

On Nov. 25, 2012, following a game between the New York Giants and the Green Bay Packers, something amazing took place as the players headed back to their locker rooms. It was reported that a middle-aged man leaned too far over the railing, lost his balance and fell. Giants' tight end Martellus Bennett saw the man plummeting 15 feet toward the ground. Bennett made his fourth reception of the day, catching the man and saving him from injury!

USA Today reported Bennett as saying, "I was doing what I usually do, moseying to the locker room and meandering around. Naturally, I just wanted to step back, but I did the righteous thing and I stepped up. I caught him, I saved his life. I tapped into my inner superhero, which I do have. I'm usually a ninja, but my Spidey-senses told me he was going to take a fall, so I saved his life." Way to step up Bennett! He admitted that naturally he would step back, but in this instance he did the "righteous" thing.

How many times have we stepped back, instead of stepping up? We may not have "Spidey-senses" in us to alert us to right and wrong, but we do have greater powers! As a believer in Jesus Christ, we have something better inside us—God's Holy Spirit! Thanks to God's Spirit, we have the ability and the power within us to step up. We have the power to love, to forgive, to help, to avoid sin, and to say and do the right things.

So have courage and step up! While you may not physically save someone's life, but you never know how God might use you spiritually. —*Rex Stump*

Go

1. What do you think of Bennett's act? Did it inspire you?
2. How many times have you been in a position to do the "right" thing and followed through on it?
3. Where can you step up let God's Spirit and power work through you?

Workout

Romans 8:11; Hebrews 13:21; 1 John 4:4

Overtime

Heavenly Father, thank You for giving me your Holy Spirit. Thank You for empowering me with the ability to make the right choices. Today I choose to step up and use your power to live righteously!

Journal

HEART OF A COMPETITOR

64

Grace and Strength

Ready

But He said to me, "My grace is sufficient for you,
for power is perfected in weakness." Therefore, I will most
gladly boast all the more about my weaknesses, so that
Christ's power may reside in me.

2 CORINTHIANS 12:9

Set

The one thing competitors strive to never be is weak! Being mentally and physically tough for your sport is a good thing. However, strength often leads to self-sufficiency and an unwillingness to admit the need for help. In fact, it often goes a step further and the coach or competitor ends up pretending. Rather than feeling vulnerable, one chooses to hide behind a mask of confidence and capability.

This negatively affects teammates as they deal with feelings of inadequacy from playing the comparison game, worship at the altar of performance and eventually learn to wear their own masks of self-sufficiency. Sadly, this not only describes some sports teams, but also some Christian circles.

We all need help, and we will never grow if we are too proud to admit it. The stakes are high! We all need God's grace, but we must admit our weakness and need in order to receive it.

Is there an area where you have been too embarrassed to admit you need help? Don't let pride stand in the way of receiving the greatest gift in the universe—God's grace. Your strength is no match for His. —Kerry O'Neill

Go

1. What skill in your sport have you avoided rather than seeking help to master?
2. Do you seek to help your teammates get better? Do you celebrate their successes?

3. Which weakness in your life could be an opportunity for God's grace and power?

Workout
Proverbs 18:12; 2 Corinthians 12:1-10; James 4:6; 1 Peter 5:5-6

Overtime
*Lord, I admit that I have avoided weakness and vulnerability.
I've tried to be self-reliant and I've fallen into the trap of
pretending and comparing. Forgive me. Soften my heart to seek
Your grace and strength in my weakness. Amen.*

Journal

65

Tough Questions

Ready

Search me, God, and know my heart; test me and
know my concerns. See if there is any offensive way in me;
lead me in the everlasting way.

PSALM 139:23-24

Set

Being on FCA staff, I have the opportunity to spend time with amazing leaders from around the world. One of my goals is to be a sponge and ask them as many questions as possible. However, very few people maximize the opportunity to ask questions. Like the Chinese Proverb says, "One who asks a question is a fool for five minutes; one who does not ask a question remains a fool forever." Asking the right questions in the right way at the right time can reveal powerful insight.

To better ourselves as Christian competitors, we must be willing to ask ourselves tough questions. This isn't questioning yourself, rather asking yourself questions. One is a matter of doubting, the other discovery. It is hard to dig into your own heart and uncover what lurks beneath the surface. Self-examination is never found at bargain prices, but it's always worth it.

Here are examples of some tough questions to start with. Let each question sink in before you rush to the next one.

Tough Questions Competitors Must Ask:

1. Do I realize it is impossible to glorify Christ and myself at the same time? *(Compete with humility)*

2. Am I doing the things that I expect of others? *(Compete with integrity)*

3. Do I pray as if nothing of eternal value will happen in the lives of others unless God does it? *(Compete with prayer)*

4. What's it like to compete as my opponent? *(Compete with authenticity)*

5. Do others experience God's love through me? *(Compete with love)*

6. Am I making others better around me? *(Compete with serving)*

Let God have complete access to your heart. Allow Him to ask you tough questions like these and mold you more into the image of Jesus Christ. —*Dan Britton*

Go

1. Do you ask yourself tough questions? If so, what?
2. As you were answering the six questions given in this reading, how did the Lord speak to you?
3. As a competitor, which areas need extra examination? Ask for God's insight in these areas.

Workout
Proverbs 1:5; 9:9; 2 Timothy 3:16

Overtime
Lord God, I want to be a life-learner. Help me to be quick to listen and slow to speak. Give me a teachable spirit. Amen.

Journal

66

Play to Your Strengths

Ready

Do not lack diligence; be fervent in spirit;
serve the Lord. Rejoice in hope; be patient in affliction;
be persistent in prayer.

ROMANS 12:11-12

Set

As a coach or athlete, you always want to flip the game to your advantage and play to your strengths. Whether on the court or the field, you look for that matchup or match ups that will allow you to play your best and gain the greatest competitive advantage.

Why wouldn't you do the same thing in your spiritual life? God is your X-factor, and what He provides for you are your spiritual strengths. When you use all that He gives you access to, then you have the competitive advantage over any challenge you face.

In Romans 12:11-12, the apostle Paul outlines five specifics that will give you poise, peace and power on the sideline and the court.

1. *Never be lacking in zeal* . . . keep your passion for what you do no matter the circumstances.

2. *Keep your spiritual fervor* . . . never lose your spiritual fire or cause someone else to lose theirs; your consistent fervency is contagious.

3. *Be joyful in hope* . . . remember your hope is not in what you do but in who you do it for.

4. *Patient in affliction* . . . God is still God in the midst of difficulties and uncertainties.

5. *Faithful in prayer* . . . this is your most powerful weapon; use it to your advantage.

Like any adversary, the enemy wants to take advantage of your weaknesses and make you forget about your strengths. These five principles are a must within any believer's arsenal. Do not forsake them. Take hold of each of them and learn to play to the strengths God has provided. —*Fleceia Comeaux*

Go

1. As an athlete, are you allowing the enemy to keep you from playing to your strengths? If so, how?
2. Have you lost your spiritual fervor or zeal because you've had a series of bad plays or games?
3. Are you no longer joyful in hope, patient in difficulties or faithful in prayer? How can you turn those things around so they will work in your favor on and off the field?

Workout

Galatians 5:22; 1 Peter 5:8

Overtime

Father, help me to never be lacking in zeal, to consistently keep my spiritual fervor, to be joyful in hope, patient in affliction and most importantly faithful in prayer. Father, show me how to better plug into Your Spirit so I can play to the strengths you provide. In Jesus' name. Amen.

Journal

_____

_____

_____

_____

_____

_____

_____

_____

67

Gold with God

Ready

For all have sinned and fall short of the glory
of God. They are justified freely by His grace through
the redemption that is in Christ Jesus.

ROMANS 3:23-24

Set

The 2012 Summer Olympics were full of excitement and surprises! There were moments of exhilaration as athletes excelled and won in an unexpected manner, and then there were moments of disappointment when the favored team failed to win gold. In spite of our predictions or expectations, results can never fully be calculated.

Olympian gymnast Gabby Douglas was expected to win on the uneven bars. But when she fell short of her goal, many of her avid followers were perplexed. The 2011 world vaulting champion gymnast McKayla Maroney was poised to walk away with Olympic gold, but ended up with silver. Instead of celebrating, many Americans were stunned with disappointment.

Spiritually speaking, many of us believe that our actions are good enough to win gold with God. But as the apostle Paul says in Romans, we all have sinned and fallen short of perfection. We make mistakes. There are deductions and flaws in our lives, proving it impossible to win gold with God.

But through His love and grace, God has made a way to be right with Him. He sent His Son Jesus Christ to this earth to live a perfect, gold-medal life and become the ultimate sacrifice for us! And Romans 3:22 tells us that by placing our faith in Jesus Christ, our mistakes are wiped out and we "win gold" with God! It's that easy. Through His forgiveness and help, we can live a spiritually-golden life! —*Rex Stump*

Go

1. Have you ever expected a win only to face defeat?
2. Are you trying to live a perfect life without God? How so?
3. Have you received God's love and grace to forgive your sins? If not, take time to do so today.

Workout

Luke 7:36-50; Romans 3

Overtime

Heavenly Father, I have fallen short and made mistakes. Forgive me. Pick me up and help me live a victorious life for You!

Journal

68

Call Timeout

Ready

He said to them, "Come away by yourselves to a remote
place and rest for a while."

MARK 6:31

Set

Have you ever been part of a game when nothing was going right?
Your opponent had the momentum, and you needed to stop it before the game was lost. What a perfect time to call timeout!

It's easy to get to a point in a game and in life where we need to
call a timeout. Sometimes we're overwhelmed by everything that
needs to be accomplished; other times we're afraid to fall behind. We
over coach, over train and even push through injuries, and eventually find ourselves burned out.

God knows we needed regular rest in order to be our best. He
has given us two gifts so we can unplug and escape: *Sabbath and sleep.*
The gift of Sabbath is a once-a-week opportunity for God to breathe
life back into our weary soul.

> Therefore, a Sabbath rest remains for God's people. For the
> person who has entered His rest has rested from his own
> works, just as God did from His (Hebrews 4:9-10).

God gives us the Sabbath to focus our mind and heart on Him
so He can reset our priorities and revitalize our soul.

Also, the gift of sleep is a process that restores and rebuilds our
health. A recent study with the Stanford University men's basketball
team showed that increased sleep dramatically improved their
shooting accuracy, speed and reaction time. They also reported better moods and less fatigue.

In vain you rise early and stay up late, toiling for food to eat—certainly He gives sleep to the one He loves (Psalm 127:1-2, abridged).

Jesus modeled how to find rest. He practiced it and taught how to find it. If we want to operate at our highest level for Him, we need to do the same. It's time we take a timeout and let God bless us with the refreshment of rest. —*Jimmy Page, Adapted from WisdomWalks Sports*

Go
1. What prevents you from receiving the gift of the Sabbath?
2. Do you get enough sleep each night? If not, what needs to change?

Workout
Psalm 23:2-3; Isaiah 40:31; Matthew 11:28-30

Overtime
Father, I confess that I have not received Your gift of rest. Give me the strength to build in proper time for You to recharge my body, mind and soul. Amen.

Journal

69

Disappointment in Competition

Ready

And not only that, but we also rejoice in our afflictions, because we know that affliction produces endurance, endurance produces proven character, and proven character produces hope. This hope will not disappoint us, because God's love has been poured out in our hearts through the Holy Spirit who was given to us.

ROMANS 5:3-5

Set

All competitors will eventually know the pain of disappointment. You put everything into preparing for the game, the competition or try outs. Although you poured yourself into practice and preparation, in the end, the outcome did not match your expectations. Or perhaps an unexpected event outside of your control changed the course of the victory or success you anticipated.

Your investment seems a waste, or perhaps you question why God would allow this defeat. Disappointment is normal; however, if we focus on ourselves, disappointment leads to frustration, discouragement and self-pity. Left unchecked, it leads to discontentment, disgruntlement and perhaps a defeated spirit. These are all enemies to the competitor and to spiritual growth.

However, when we offer our disappointments up to God, He will use it for our good and His glory (Romans 8:28). God wants us to rejoice in the midst of disappointment. How can we rejoice? Because we know God is using the disappointment to produce endurance.

We endure by trusting God, and even though disappointed, we continue to show up to practice, execute each drill with a positive attitude, and remain faithful to our coaches and teammates. God's Word promises that endurance will eventually produce hope. This is a hope that does not disappoint. This is God's certain hope that He is with you no matter what, that He will use the good and the bad for

your good and His glory. You can truly rejoice no matter what comes!
—*Janet Turnbough*

Go

1. Can you think of a time you experienced disappointment in competition? How did you handle it?
2. When you experience disappointment in the future, will you take it to God?
3. How can you endure after experiencing defeat?

Workout

Psalm 147:11; Romans 8:28-30

Overtime

Lord, You are faithful. You are near when I experience success and when I am brokenhearted in disappointment. Teach me to rejoice in victory as well as in defeat. Help me to bring them both to You, knowing You will use every outcome for my good and Your glory! Amen.

Journal

70

My House

Ready

And the things that you have heard from me
among many witnesses, commit these to faithful men
who will be able to teach others also.

2 TIMOTHY 2:2, NKJV

Set

I think we would all agree that Moses was a man of God. Though he had his mishaps along the way, God had this testimony about him, "He is faithful in all My house." So what caused God to say this about Moses? Well, not only did he lead God's chosen people out of their slavery in Egypt, build the Tabernacle (the place where God's glory would dwell) and receive from God's hand the Ten Commandments, he also did not neglect to make disciples.

Moses was faithful to pass on the word of God to the next generation and reminded the people of God's mighty acts on their behalf. He invested in the leaders among the people, specifically a young man named Joshua. Moses noticed his heart for God and took this young man under his wing.

Undoubtedly Moses taught with words but also with his life. Joshua learned much from his mentor including how to lead and serve people and about God's character; His faithfulness, lovingkindness, and mercy. Things he would soon learn firsthand.

After Moses' death, God appointed Joshua to be Israel's new leader. God spoke to him saying, "As I was with Moses, so I will be with you . . . Only be strong and very courageous that you may observe to do according to all the law which Moses my servant commanded you." I'm sure this brought Joshua great comfort to know that in the same way he witnessed God act in Moses' life, God would show Himself to be just as faithful in his. And we know the end of his story. Like Moses, Joshua too was indeed faithful. He was victorious in bringing

the people into the land of Promise. His famous last words still echo in our homes today, "As for me and my house, we will serve the Lord."
—*Alex Hagler*

Go

1. Have you ever been discipled? (If not, seek out someone whose walk with the Lord you respect and admire and ask him or her to disciple you.)
2. If you have been discipled, what impact did that relationship have on you as a Christian competitor?
3. How can you continue the legacy of that person's faithfulness in the competitive realm?

Workout
Psalm 145:4; Matthew 28:18-20; 1 Thessalonians 2:8; Hebrews 4:12

Overtime
Father, Please help me see the opportunities to be discipled and to disciple others on my team and in my community. Amen.

Journal

_____

_____

_____

_____

_____

_____

_____

_____

_____

_____

_____

71

Not Top Ten

Ready

And My people who are called by My name humble themselves, pray and seek My face, and turn from their evil ways, then I will hear from heaven, forgive their sin, and heal their land.

2 CHRONICLES 7:14

Set

Many of us hear and understand the phrase "Top Ten" when it comes to athletic highlights shown on television. The "Top Ten" plays are always the talk of the day, but what about those "Not Top Ten" plays? The highlights of an athlete's most embarrassing moments caught on tape. These sure-footed, strong and highly talented athletes recorded making big-time bloopers. Talk about being humbled!

In 2 Chronicles 32—33, there is a story of a father and his son, both kings who are humbled by their mistakes. The first king Hezekiah seemed to be on the right track in leading his nation toward God. The problem occurred when he prayed for healing, and in his pride he never thanked God for the miracle that occurred. God humbled Hezekiah; the king repented and got things right with God.

King Manasseh replaced worshipping God with the sin of sorcery, witchcraft and consulting psychics. Manasseh ignored God's warnings, so God allowed an opposing army to defeat Manasseh. They put a ring through his nose, bound him in chains and led him away to a foreign land. Manasseh sincerely humbled himself to God and asked for forgiveness.

Just like some athletes, these kings experienced a "Not Top Ten" moment in life. I believe we all have "Not Top Ten" moments. If you find yourself humbled by a mistake, pray for forgiveness and turn back to God. Don't allow a "Not Top Ten" moment to define your life. With God's help, pick yourself up, dust yourself off and move forward, taking with you a valuable lesson. —*Rex Stump*

Go

1. What is one of your "Not Top Ten" moments in life? What did you learn from the experience?
2. Did you humble yourself before God? Why or why not?
3. How can you avoid future "Not Top Ten" moments?

Workout

2 Chronicles 32—33; Psalm 147:5-7

Overtime

*Heavenly Father, forgive me for my pride. Forgive me
for the times I tried to rule my life. I have been humbled by
mistakes, and I need your help to get back up. Help me today
to live in a way that pleases You!*

Journal

_____

_____

_____

_____

_____

_____

_____

_____

_____

_____

_____

_____

_____

_____

_____

_____

72

Get Up

Ready

Get up, for this matter is your responsibility,
and we support you. Be strong and take action!

EZRA 10:4

Set

Former Ohio State University coach Jim Tressel cheated . . . well, at least according to the NCAA rules he did. What actually happened was some of his players cheated, and he failed to report their misbehavior, making him guilty too. Scandalous!

In the Old Testament book of Ezra, we read that the Israelites also cheated. God had specifically told them not to marry foreign wives, but many of them did so anyway. So they, too, found themselves in the middle of a scandal.

Both of these situations may look rather nominal to most. What is the big deal? So a few players made some money for selling tickets. So what? Or somebody took an oath to love someone else till death do they part? Come on! These seem like good ideas. The problem is we don't make the rules; we just suffer the consequences after breaking them.

Ezra 10:4 gives us some great advice in the midst of a controversy. First, we are to take ownership of our part in breaking the rules. Second, we are to support each other in the midst of a scandal. And third, we are to get up and take action. Don't wallow. Don't whine. Move on.

The Israelites eventually followed these instructions, and God honored them for their obedience. None of us are above scandalous behavior. And the athletic field seems to be an opportune place to sin. The question is, will we take the advice given in Scripture or will we make excuses? I say, "Get up and take action!" —*Clay Elliott*

Go

1. What rules in athletics seem unfair?
2. What are some of the excuses you could be tempted to use to justify your breaking of these rules?
3. What are the benefits to obeying God's rules?

Workout

Exodus 20:1-17; Ezra 10

Overtime

Father, I realize I don't make the rules, and even though some don't make sense, help me to be more obedient. And when I do break them, give me the strength to get up, ask for forgiveness and go forward. In Jesus' name I pray. Amen.

Journal

73

Coming Back After Injury

Ready

Therefore, since Christ suffered in the flesh, equip
yourselves also with the same resolve—because the one
who suffered in the flesh has finished with sin.

1 PETER 4:1

Set

Who has more confidence about recovering from injury, the one who
has never been hurt or the player who has come through the pain and
has found renewed strength? If the answer seems obvious, you may
have never been injured.

The apostle Peter makes mention of suffering and its results in
the above Scripture. He's not saying that after we've suffered that we're
somehow exempt from making moral mistakes, rather suffering changes
our mindset and leads us to live for more than physical gratification.

Before we've suffered any significant injury, many of us play a little tentatively in dangerous situations. There is a latent fear that if we
risk a possible injury, we can never recover or play the same again.
However, in the player who has suffered and recovered, that indecision
and fear is overcome by the assurance that even if this daring play
leads to pain, he can come through it to compete even more strongly.

As you compete today, play with strength, courage and tenacity.
Don't be intimidated by the potential injury that you imagine could
wreck your playing career. And to those of you who have come
through injury, who have suffered in the flesh, loan some courage to
your teammates and play with great passion. —*Roger Lipe*

Go

1. How have the injuries which you have suffered led you to
   a greater confidence and a more passionate approach to
   competition?

2. What does it mean to share in Christ's sufferings?
3. How does experiencing such sufferings help you overcome temptation, habitual sins and other trials?

Workout
1 Corinthians 10:13; James 1:12; 1 Peter 1:6

Overtime
Lord, I pray for the strength to bear the burden of Your cross with courage and assurance, knowing You are always with me. Help me to use my experiences to encourage other believers to do the same. Amen.

Journal

74

What Have You Done with the Son of God?

Ready

After three days, they found Him in the temple
complex sitting among the teachers, listening to them and
asking them questions. . . . When His parents saw Him [Jesus],
they were astonished, and His mother said to Him,
"Son, why have You treated us like this? Your father and I have
been anxiously searching for You."

LUKE 2:46,48

Set

Jesus and his parents were in Jerusalem for the Passover. After they
had celebrated the feast, Mary and Joseph began to pack their belong-
ings and head home after the festival. A day had passed when they realized Jesus was not with them on the road. They began to ask around
and frantically look for him; when they could not find him amongst
the people in their camp, they decided to go back to the city and look
around there.

You have to wonder on their journey back to the city if they might
have asked, "What have we done with the Son of God?" Their worry
and concern was more than that of the typical parent. It was an over-
whelming feeling of loss and confusion because they could not remember what they had done with God's Son. For three days they
asked everywhere until they heard him speaking and teaching in the
synagogue. He was exactly where he should have been, in the presence
of God and amongst God's people.

So let me ask you, is Jesus where He should be in your life or do
you much like Mary and Joseph need to ask, "What have I done with
the Son of God?"

They had traveled for a full day before they realized he was not
with them. How long have you gone before you realize He is not with

you? Do you allow Him access to every area of your life, including athletics? Is He guiding you as you compete for His glory and honor or have you left Him behind, thinking you don't need Him in your sport?

Jesus' parents also began to ask the others among their relatives and friends if they knew where He was. Have you asked others where He might be? And when it was all said and done they had left no stone unturned trying to find Him. What lengths will you go to be with Jesus so He can guide you in life and sport? —*Fleceia Comeaux*

Go

1. So, what have you done with the Son of God? Is He still present in your sport?
2. Can you still see His hand on you as you compete, coach or perform?
3. How long has it been since you acknowledged Him in your sport or gave Him praise for your accomplishments?

Workout
Luke 2:41-50; 11:9-13

Overtime
Father let me stay in a place where I can see You. And if I should journey away from Your side, let me be like Mary and Joseph leaving no stone unturned until I find You. In Jesus' name. Amen.

Journal

_____

_____

_____

_____

_____

_____

_____

_____

75

Positive Goals

Ready

I pursue as my goal the prize promised by God's
heavenly call in Christ Jesus.

PHILIPPIANS 3:14

Set

Goals not only give competitors and teams purpose and direction, but they serve as a reminder of the potential rewards that await ahead of all of the hard work and training. One essential element to achieving a goal is that it must be stated in a positive manner. You see, the Lord created a part of our brain called the reticular activating system (RAS). One of the functions of this system is to filter incoming stimuli and determine where one focuses attention. And when it comes to setting goals, the RAS plays part in how they're interpreted.

For example, a football place kicker can word his goal one of two ways. Either "my goal is to make this kick" or "my goal is to not miss this kick." They may seem pretty similar, but there is a huge difference. Your RAS will choose to focus on one thing. In the first case, the focus is on making the kick. In the second, it is on missing the kick, even though the goal is to not miss it. The last thing a competitor should be thinking about is the potential of failure because our brains will capture that thought, increasing the likelihood of a disappointing outcome.

The apostle Paul stated that his goal regarding God was "to know Him" (Philippians 3:10). The thought of "knowing God" and His calling was stuck in his head rather than the idea of "not missing out" on his relationship with God. And Paul pursued that goal and God's promises (v. 14) with a reckless abandon. So, begin stating your spiritual and physical goals in the positive, allowing the intricate brain process the Lord has equipped you with to focus on reaching them. —*Kerry O'Neill*

Go

1. What is one goal you have for sports? For your relationship with God? For your life?
2. Do you have any goals that are stated in the negative that need changing?
3. Are you, like Paul, pursuing the goal of knowing God and His promises? '

Workout

Proverbs 21:5; Matthew 6:33; Philippians 3:10-14

Overtime

Father, thank You for the amazing way you created my mind and body. Give me the wisdom to set goals that will bring You honor and bring me closer to You. Amen.

Journal

76

Beyond Sight

Ready
For we walk by faith, not by sight.

2 CORINTHIANS 5:7

Set
Amidst the small beautiful city of Guarapari, Brazil, Derek Rabelo's father prayed that his son would become a famous professional surfer. His father named his son after the legendary Pipeline surfer Derek Ho, the embodiment of his dream. Unfortunately on May 25, 1992, his prayers seemed unanswered when Derek was born blind.

Seventeen years later, Derek decided that despite his blindness he still wanted to surf and that he wanted to surf Pipeline on the North Shore of Oahu, Hawaii. Through the encouragement of his parents, best friend and surf coach, Derek embarked on a three-year journey of grueling mental, physical and spiritual training to accomplish his goal. Knowing it wasn't an easy feat, Derek reflected on the blessing God had granted, seeing his surfing ability as a gift directly from Him.*

Being blind isn't an obstacle when you have the right attitude and a good measure of faith. Derek's story teaches us that the best journeys in life are walked out by faith and not by sight. —*Joe Matera*

Go
1. Can you imagine participating in your sport without eyesight? How would you train?
2. What spiritual steps can you take to walk more by faith and less by sight?
3. How can having blind faith move you to become more courageous?

Workout
Joshua 1:7; 2 Corinthians 4:18; Hebrews 11:1

Overtime

Lord Jesus, thank you for giving me courage and a vision beyond what my eyes can physically see. Help my life reflect complete faith in You. Amen.

(Derek and his story is the subject of the upcoming documentary *Beyond Sight*.)

Journal

77

The Ring

Ready

I also consider everything to be a loss in view of the surpassing
value of knowing Christ Jesus my Lord. . . . Pursue as my goal the
prize promised by God's heavenly call in Christ Jesus.

PHILIPPIANS 3:8,14

Set

In June of 2005, Tom Brady sat on top of the football world. With
three Super Bowl rings on his fingers, you might think he had it all:
fame, fortune, success. But deep inside Tom knew something was
missing. He said, "Why do I have three Super Bowl Rings and still
think . . . it's gotta be more than this." He had fulfilled his dreams and
yet was still empty.

Vince Lombardi once said, "Winning isn't everything. It's the
only thing." And many coaches and athletes today agree. Wanting to
win isn't a bad thing. But when the pursuit of "the ring" becomes the
ultimate thing, we've got a problem. Paul wanted to win, but Philippians shows he wanted to make sure it was the right prize—one that
would be worth the effort and sacrifice.

Paul knew that his box full of trophies was worth nothing compared with knowing Jesus. He knew his "rings" couldn't satisfy him like
living for Jesus could. God never designed the "rings" in our life to satisfy us or give us our identity. When we put all our energy and passion
into chasing rings, success or records, we'll be disappointed and empty.

Jesus is the only prize that satisfies; He's the only thing worth
pursuing with our whole heart. When we know Christ and experience
His love, we are satisfied. And I promise you, you'll never say, "it's
gotta be more than this."

Stop chasing after the rings of temporary pleasure and success.
Stop searching for substitutes that never satisfy. Keep your eyes on
the prize. —*Jimmy Page, Adapted from WisdomWalks Sports*

Go

1. What are the "rings" that you are pursuing?
2. What things do you desire more passionately than Christ?
3. How can you keep your eyes focused on the "real" prize in life?

Workout

Matthew 5:6; 6:19-21; Hebrews 12:1-2

Overtime

Father, I pray that You will change my heart to love and pursue things that will last forever. I know that worldly success looks good from the outside, but leaves me empty on the inside. Help me to refocus on Jesus, the only prize that satisfies. Amen.

Journal

HEART OF A COMPETITOR

78

Express Yourself

Ready

My mouth will tell about Your righteousness and Your salvation all day long, though I cannot sum them up.

PSALM 71:15

Set

I don't think I've ever seen an athlete turn down an interview. Have you ever seen a coach be short of words during a press conference? Typically most athletes and coaches enjoy expressing their opinions, strategies and explanations of game-day decisions.

We, too, have the opportunity every day to express ourselves by the way we talk. Whether you are being interviewed or not, you will eventually express yourself with words. Besides our words, our actions also reveal who we are on the inside. So my question is, "what message are you expressing?"

In Psalm 71, the author asserts that "I will praise [God] more and more!" (v. 14) The author also says, "I will proclaim Your righteousness" (v. 16) to others. He doesn't put it on his "to do" list or say "I ought to." He says "I will." That's called personal responsibility. That's called making the choice.

Too often we allow people, excuses and possible appointments to dictate our schedules and our actions.

We need to stop allowing others to keep us silent when it comes to expressing our faith. Like the psalmist, we must make the proclamation and the choice to express our thanks to God!

Have you ever been to a store that sets out free food samples? Those free samples entice you to buy the product. They are examples and expressions of what you could choose to purchase. We are living "samples" and Christ "taste tests" to this world. Do not doubt what God can do or say through you! Your words and actions are a living expression of His love. So every day make it a habit to openly express your thanks to God! —*Rex Stump*

Go

1. What kind of example are you setting by your words and your actions?
2. Have you ever allowed others to keep you silent regarding your faith? Explain.
3. How can you better express a thankful heart to God?

Workout

Psalms 71; 96:1-3; 121

Overtime

Heavenly Father, thank You for all that you have done for me! Thank You for all that you have given to me! Help me to be a living expression of thanksgiving to You!

Journal

79

Change the Atmosphere

Ready

I labor for this, striving with His strength that
works powerfully in me.

COLOSSIANS 1:29

Set

It is not enough to know who you are; you must also know what you possess. The apostle Peter always knew who he was. Peter always understood that he had a presence about him and knew that his relationship with Jesus was different than any of the others. From the time Jesus said to him, "on this rock I will build my church," (Matthew 16:18) Peter's life would never be the same.

But Peter struggled with this new reality. Sometimes it's easier to be who people think we are, than to step into who God says we are. Like Peter we must come to a time of transition when we switch from fear, anger and denial to redemption, salvation and power!

When Peter made the switch and allowed God to unlock the potential of his presence, he began to experience God in a way he had never known before. Peter's very presence, or rather the thick presence of God on him, began to change the atmosphere around him. Whether he spoke or passed by, the power of God was amazing every time he showed up.

As a competitor, there is nothing more exciting than being in a heated battle with an opponent in their home arena, stadium or gym. You flow with every movement, seemingly effortless. But just before you know it, the opponent gains the momentum and the crowd goes wild. Your coach calls a play designed just for you, you execute with success and the crowd is silenced. You have just changed the atmosphere! If a mere play of an athlete can change the atmosphere, how much more can the power of God working through you. —*Fleceia Comeaux*

Go

1. Have you ever experienced a game when a single play changed the entire atmosphere? How did it feel?
2. What can you do to change the spiritual atmosphere within your team, on the court/field or in your school?
3. How can you increase your God confidence so that His power and presence is constantly displayed in you?

Workout

Romans 1:16; 2 Timothy 1:7

Overtime

God, thank You for Your desire to infiltrate my very being. Change the atmosphere in me so that through Your power, I can change the atmosphere around me. In Jesus' name. Amen.

Journal

_____

_____

_____

_____

_____

_____

_____

_____

_____

_____

_____

_____

_____

_____

80

Eyes on the Target

Ready

And climbing out of the boat, Peter started walking on
water and came toward Jesus. But when he saw the
strength of the wind, he was afraid. And beginning to
sink he cried out, "Lord save me!"

MATTHEW 14:30

Set

One of the oldest acrostics in basketball is B.E.E.F. The "B" is for
"balance." The first "E" is for "eyes on target." The second "E" is for
"elbow straight." And the "F" is for "follow through." Each one is
important, but plenty of shots go into the basket even though the
shooter is off balance, has bent elbows or doesn't follow through.
But seldom will a ball find the hoop if the shooter's eyes aren't fixed
on the target. Each player has his or her own target in their respec-
tive sport. A pitcher in baseball must get the ball over the plate. A
swimmer needs to reach the other end of the pool. A pole vaulter has
to clear the crossbar.

As important as goals are within sports, at the heart of every
great Christian competitor should be the discipline of focusing on a
greater purpose. Just look at what taking ones' eyes off the target
produced in the life of the disciple Peter in Matthew 14. He wanted
to walk on water with Jesus and did so until he shifted his eyes from
Christ to the fierce wind. He became fearful and began to sink.

Likewise, we will start sinking in our lives if we choose to focus on the tumult that surrounds us. We must allow the Holy Spirit
to be our guide, reminding us that with Christ, all is well with our
souls. No matter the final score, injury or pressure, if we fix our
eyes on Christ, our target, and trust His faithful provision, we will
be able to accomplish His purposes, both in our game and our life.
—*Charlotte Smith*

Go

1. What is your ultimate target?
2. When pressure comes, do you tend to stay focused or become distracted?
3. How can you better keep yourself from shifting your eyes off God?

Workout

Luke 2:30, John 10:27, 1 Corinthians 16:13

Overtime

Lord, keep me grounded in my faith. Help me to keep my eyes lifted to the hills from where all my help comes. Help me to always fix my eyes on You so that my faith will never waver. Amen.

Journal

81

Together

Ready

For as the body is one and has many parts, and all the parts of that body, though many, are one body—so also is Christ.

1 CORINTHIANS 12:12

Set

Former University of Southern California quarterback Matt Barkley will forever be remembered by the cardinal and gold faithful for rewriting the USC and Pac-12 record books during his four years at Southern Cal. But in a spirit of humility, Barkley realizes those accomplishments would have never been possible without his Trojan teammates.

"Football is such a unique sport because of the team aspect of the game," Barkley said. "Every play there has to be 11 guys doing the exact right thing or else it won't work. But, when all those things do come together, all the hard work you put together as teammates collides in a perfect play; it's one of the most exhilarating things I've experienced."

It's the perfect analogy for what Paul was explaining in 1 Corinthians 12. Each of us plays a certain position or role on our team because of the abilities we possess. Alone, we'd never be able to reach the same accomplishments as when those abilities are combined with a team. And the same applies to our responsibilities as a Christ-follower. We each play an important role in doing God's kingdom work with the spiritual gifts we've been given. And when we team up with other believers, He is able to do even mightier works through us.

The key is knowing your role. So, how can you use your spiritual gifts on your team? As an encourager or maybe a servant-leader? Just as you're responsible for fulfilling your athletic role on your team, be committed to fill God's role for His Kingdom. When your gifts are combined with the gifts of those around you, the Spirit of the Lord will be alive and active and your impact unstoppable. —*Clay Meyer*

Go

1. What role do you fill on your team?
2. Take a moment to assess the spiritual gifts God has given you. How can you use those to better serve on Christ's team?
3. What parallels are there between trying to do too much alone in your sport and for Christ? How do they compare? What are their results?

Workout

1 Corinthians 1:10; 12; Ephesians 4:1-16

Overtime

Father, God, thank You for giving me unique gifts and talents to fill a specific role on my team in Your Kingdom. I pray for wisdom to know how to best do my part to reflect You in my life. In Your precious Son's name. Amen.

Journal

82

Single-Handed

Ready

God has put the body together, giving greater honor to the less honorable, so that there would be no division in the body, but that the members would have the same concern for each other.

1 CORINTHIANS 12:24-25

Set

Have you ever been guilty of trying to coach "single-handedly"? If you have, you know from experience that it's not the most efficient or effective way to get things done. As a young head coach, I had the attitude that if it were going to get done the way I wanted, I had to do it myself.

Looking back, it's not too hard for me to see a little pride and ego in my methods. I wanted to prove that I was capable of getting the job done. Little did I realize that not only was I wearing myself out, I was also denying my coaching staff the opportunity to grow and develop their own coaching skills. As I matured, I began to understand that trying to do things by myself would always limit the scope of what could be done and make me old at an early age.

The apostle Paul reminds us that we need each other. Yes, we can accomplish great things with the gifts God has given us, but we can do so much more if we connect our gifts with the gifts of others. When the people of God come together as a team, watch out! There is something about a common goal that naturally connects people. This is true in athletics, business, church and ministry. We might call it having "good chemistry." What actually happens is we stop thinking about ourselves and start thinking about how we can get the job done. We stop trying to do it all and simply begin to do our part.

God intended us to be unified. Regardless of where God has placed us, He has others ready to join the team as we pursue our common goal. Don't make the mistake of trying to run the race on your own. —*Charles Gee*

Go

1. When have you been guilty of trying to accomplish an athletic goal single-handedly?
2. What unique gifts has God given you?
3. What is the best team of which you have been part? Why?

Workout

John 17:20-23; Philippians 2:1-3

Overtime

Lord, forgive me for trying to do it all by myself. Teach me to trust the teammates You put beside me each day. Amen

Journal

83

Don't Mess Up a Good Thing

Ready

Wisdom is better than weapons of war,
but one sinner can destroy much good.

ECCLESIASTES 9:18

Set

Imagine a football stadium full of excited fans. The home team is losing by six points. It's fourth down and they have the ball with less than a minute left on the game clock. The offensive line provides great protection as the quarterback drops back and throws the ball to his receiver in the end zone. It's good, touchdown!

Wait, there is a flag on the field. It appears that an offensive lineman was called for holding. The touchdown doesn't count. All it took was one mistake and a would-be victory is out of reach. No matter the good done prior, it is this one poor decision that has cost the home team the game.

In Ecclesiastes 9:18 we are reminded that "one" sinner can destroy much that is good. To sin is to miss the mark, to mess up. We are all guilty of making bad decisions and have the potential to destroy much good. And it just takes one. One sinful act can really make a mess of something good.

One spouse wanders away and suddenly an entire family is a mess. One student acts up and the teacher punishes a whole class. One driver wanders out of his lane and destroys the life of an innocent passenger. One person making morally bad choices can mess up a hundred would-be good things.

The writer of Ecclesiastes says that having wisdom (the ability to make great choices) is better than a weapon (something that ultimately makes you feel powerful). It is through wisdom we find great power to turn from sin. And where does wisdom come from? Straight from the source: God. So if you don't want sin to destroy your life or the lives of others, get wise! —*Rex Stump*

Go

1. Have you ever had a single bad choice mess up a good thing?
2. How would you define "godly wisdom"?
3. How can you make more of an effort to gain godly wisdom?

Workout

Psalm 111:10; James 1:5-6

Overtime

Heavenly Father, I don't want to be mastered by sin. I pray for your wisdom to avoid bad decisions. Help me from destroying "much good." Amen.

Journal

84

Taking Care of Business

Ready

Love the Lord your God with all your heart, with all your soul
and with all your mind and with all your strength.

MARK 12:30

Set

For most of my life I have had a problem with these words: *Just do your
best. What is most important is having a good attitude and giving your best effort. It's not whether you win or lose, it's how you play the game.*

It always seemed to me that these words lack a competitive spirit,
like something a mom says to her child who has no chance of winning. But I've been absolutely wrong! It occurred to me recently how
few things in sports are within our control. During a basketball game,
I cannot control the referees, the crowd, my teammates, opponents or
whether I have a record-breaking game or not. But, I can control my
attitude and my effort.

Think about it. I can give 100 percent effort and have the best attitude in 10 games and my performance will be different each time
based on other variables. I cannot control every aspect of my performance or the results. Nor can I control the attitude and effort of others,
only my own.

That being true, I should only be judged by those things which I
have complete control over—my attitude and effort during the game.
The same is true in life. What should my attitude be like? "Make your
own attitude that of Christ Jesus" (Philippians 2:5). Effort? "Whatever
you do, do it enthusiastically, as something done for the Lord and not
for men" (Colossians 3:23).

Attitude and effort are personal choices that cannot be con-
trolled by other people or circumstances without my permission. I
have the sole responsibility to make sure they line up with the words
of Christ and no one can change that. —*Kerry O'Neill*

Go

1. What are some things over which you have no control that distract you?
2. What would you consider to be a "true win" for you during training or competition?
3. How can you improve your attitude and effort?

Workout

Philippians 2:1-8; Colossians 3:23-24

Overtime

Lord, I confess that I have focused on things that I cannot control. Thank You that I don't have to perform for You or try to impress You. Help me to focus on giving my best attitude and effort to please You. Amen.

Journal

85

Remain in Me

Ready
I am the vine; you are the branches. The one who remains
in Me and I in him produces much fruit, because you can
do nothing without Me. . . . If you remain in Me and My
words remain in you, ask whatever you want and it will be done
for you. My Father is glorified by this: that you produce
much fruit and prove to be My disciples.

JOHN 15:5,7-8

Set
In John 15, Jesus is giving a final charge to his disciples about staying connected to the true vine. He encourages, reiterates and implores them to stay connected to Him. I often find it unbelievably significant when Christ repeats himself. There is a fundamental principle that He is trying to relay to the people of God and specifically His disciples.

As the text unfolds, three promises are identified as we remain in Him: we will produce much fruit, we can ask whatever we want and it will be done, and we will glorify the Father.

What athlete or coach doesn't want to produce fruit? You don't work out or practice not to produce, you do it with a goal in mind. Who doesn't want their prayers answered? When you pray over your season or your team, do you sincerely want God to answer? Yes!

And which one of us does not have a desire to glorify the Father during our performance? Your effort, work and striving in sport and life must end in His glory. When we do not remain in Him, we are setting ourselves up for failure. I don't know about you, but I choose to stay connected to the "Vine" and receive all the benefits that follow.

To remain means to continue in the same state. You have too much at stake as an athlete and believer to be detached from the Father at any time and in any way. Remain in Him, and let His Word remain in you. —*Fleceia Comeaux*

Go

1. Are you remaining in Christ throughout your season?
2. Is God's Word remaining in you as you coach, teach or perform? Why or why not?
3. What type of fruit are you producing? Are you producing fruit that will last, or are you just competing and coaching for the temporary rewards?

Workout
Psalm 119:9-11; 1 John 2:5-6

Overtime
Father it is Your desire that I remain in You and Your Word remain in me. Please help me to stay close to the things that bring me true wisdom, power and peace. Let my actions reflect Your principles, and let my decisions reflect Your heart. In Jesus' name. Amen.

Journal

86

Giving Your All

Ready

Summoning His disciples, He said to them, "I assure
you: This poor widow has put in more than all those giving
to the temple treasury. For they all gave out of their
surplus, but she out of her poverty has put in everything
she possessed—all she had to live on."

MARK 12:43-44

Set

There are many things that I count as a privilege in my athletic career. Playing football for Appalachian State, beating then-No. 5 University of Michigan and winning two Division I FCS national championships are at the top of the list.

But the greatest privilege that I've had was the opportunity to play for Coach Jerry Moore. He is a man of faith, integrity and passion. He had a slogan that we lived by: "What are you willing to give up?" His giving character fueled me and my teammates to be men who gave our all for what we believed in and it showed on and off the field.

Jesus is attracted to those who give their all, like the poor widow mentioned in Mark 12. She gave all that she had monetarily. She laid her entire livelihood down, believing that it would make a difference. It wasn't the amount as it compared to others or her circumstance that determined what she would give. Out of a selfless commitment to something larger than herself she gave everything that she had, knowing she was being faithful to her calling.

When circumstances get tough and the odds are against you, what you are willing to give will make a difference in your life. It shows the level of your commitment to a cause greater than yourself, inspiring others to do the same. So, what are you willing to give for your sport or better yet, your Savior? —*Blake Elder*

Go

1. Do your teammates recognize you as a giver or a taker?
2. Do you tend to let the negative circumstances and momentum determine whether you give your all?
3. How can you prepare yourself to not withhold what you should give physically and spiritually?

Workout

Proverbs 11:24-25; Mark 6:33-44; 2 Corinthians 9:6-11

Overtime

Lord, thank You for giving Your best to me in Your Son, Jesus. I see that I am to be a giver, both on and off the field. I pray, in the name of Jesus, that You would give me the strength to give all that I have to represent You in all circumstances. Amen.

Journal

87

Desiring and Doing

Ready

Instead, remain faithful to the LORD your God,
as you have done to this day.

JOSHUA 23:8

Set

Reidy Priddy (men's volleyball) and Donny Robinson (BMX) are
Olympic athletes whose field of competition receives little attention.
These athletes are faithful in their commitment to Jesus Christ and
their sport. They fully understand what it's like to work at something
with all their hearts, being enthusiastically committed to winning, for
the glory of God. But these two men also know that their desire must
be accompanied by action.

In Numbers 13, we are introduced to Caleb, somebody just like
Priddy and Robinson. Caleb didn't receive much notice and basically
stood in the shadow of people who received greater attention. He was
one of the 12 spies that brought a correct report to Moses about the
Promised Land of Canaan. He wasn't of Jewish background, but his
faith was solid in their God. He was faithful, knowing he was working
for God and not men, and his actions proved it!

After 38 years of wandering the desert and seven years of conquer-
ing the Promised Land, Caleb was ready to possess the land promised
to him. In Joshua 14, Caleb approached Joshua and requested the opportunity to attack and possess the Promised Land. Caleb was 85 years
old, 20 years past retirement. He wasn't collecting retirement; he was
enthusiastically serving God and kicking down the gates of Hebron
and moving his family into a new home! His desire was accompanied
by doing.

We can learn from Caleb and these athletes that having your
name in the spotlight is not a priority. What matters is a life of disciplined action with a focus on doing for God, not man. So, make sure
your desires are accompanied by action that honors Him! —*Rex Stump*

Go

1. Are you faithful to your sport regardless of whether you get praise from others or not?
2. Do you look to others or to God to affirm your faith?
3. Do your actions accompany your desire to live and work for God? If not, why not?

Workout

Numbers 13; Deuteronomy 6:5

Overtime

Heavenly Father, help me focus on doing for You and not praise from man. I pray that my spiritual and athletic desires will be accompanied by actions that honor You. Amen.

Journal

_____

_____

_____

_____

_____

_____

_____

_____

_____

_____

_____

_____

_____

_____

88

What Pushes You?

Ready

Whatever you do, do it enthusiastically, as something
done for the Lord and not for men.

COLOSSIANS 3:23

Set

During the course of a few short years in the MLB, Los Angeles
Dodgers pitcher Clayton Kershaw has already become a household
name. Winning the 2011 NL Cy Young Award, Kershaw has joined
the ranks of all-time Dodger greats such as Orel Hershiser and
Sandy Koufax.

Even though he is known as being an easygoing guy off the
field, this hard-throwing southpaw flips a switch when stepping on
the mound. He becomes a bulldog, pitching with tenacity and inten-
sity. Kershaw feels he is called to so he plays according to one of his
favorite Bible verses, Colossians 3:23.

Kershaw realizes that his faith is reflected on the field through
displaying such a competitive nature. He knows that God has given
him a talent, but that he has to work at directing the part he can
control: his passion and enthusiasm. And with this attitude, Kershaw takes the mound every fifth day of the season and pitches for
God's glory, leaving the results up to the One who put him there.
He trusts that no matter the outcome, he has given his all and left
nothing on the field.

As Christian competitors we sweat, bleed, cry and fight
through pain with fierce determination. Not for ourselves, not for
our team, not for our coach, but for the Lord. So are you doing
that today? Are others seeing Christ through the way you compete? Are you focusing your energy on the field for God's glory and
not that of man? Don't just give your all, but give your all for your
Lord. —*Clay Meyer*

Go

1. What motivates you to play or coach your sport?
2. What does Colossians 3:23 mean to you? How can you apply these words to the sport you play or coach?
3. How can you encourage your teammates or the athletes you coach to compete for the Lord with everything they have?

Workout

Romans 14:8; Ephesians 6:6-8; Colossians 3:17

Overtime

Father, I pray that as a competitor I would give everything I have for Your glory. Whether in or out of season, I desire to use the abilities and talents You've blessed me with to make Your name known. In all I do, Lord, let me honor You. Amen.

Journal

89

Linger Longer

Ready

Where can I go to escape Your Spirit? Where can
I flee from Your presence?

PSALM 139:7

Set

Unfortunately, as athletes and coaches we often approach devotions
as something that needs to get done due to our "conquer it" attitude.
Something like this: *"I rise. I read. I am done!"* Now we can get on with
the day. It becomes an action item that gets checked off the to-do list,
because we love the feeling of accomplishment. Our mindset toward
devotions is like taking medicine or eating spinach, something that
we *have to* do instead of *long to* do!

Devotions become all about us—what we can get out of it and
how much we need it. Yes, we do desperately need it, but we also need
to realize that God longs for us to be with Him. The Lord delights
when we sit at His feet each day and linger in His presence. Stopping
the chaos of the day by stepping away from all the clutter and being
consumed by His love is a non-negotiable.

Too many people go through the motions. No spiritual grit. No
investment made for the long term. When we think survival, our devotions become a matter of just getting us through the day. We're not
thinking what's down the road. We're running on spiritual fumes instead of having a full tank. Soaking in God's presence daily moves us
from spiritual surviving to spiritual thriving.

Lingering longer allows us to hear God's voice. There will always
be an opportunity to pour out what the Lord has poured in. He will
always use our extra soaking for His work. But we need to stop the
rushing, drop to our knees or fall on our face and soak in His glori-
ous presence. Sit at the feet of Jesus and wait for Him to speak. We
need to listen to the Holy Spirit instead of filling the time with our
words. Linger in His presence and find out what's on God's heart.

We need to STOP—DROP—SOAK. STOP daily; DROP before the Lord; and SOAK in His presence. Stopping is our discipline; dropping is our posture; and soaking is our worship. Extend your time with the Savior and enjoy His presence! —*Dan Britton*

Go

1. Have you soaked in God's presence before? Have you made some extended time to stop, drop and soak?
2. What about your quiet time can you change to listen better?
3. How can soaking in God help with the stress you face as a competitor?

Workout
Psalms 27:14; 62:5

Overtime
Lord, help me to linger longer in Your presence today. Open my ears and heart to hear from Your Spirit. Amen.

Journal

90

Finish the Race

Ready

**I have fought the good fight, I have finished the race,
I have kept the faith.**

2 TIMOTHY 4:7

Set

Less than halfway into the 1968 Mexico City Olympic marathon, Tanzanian runner John Stephen Akhwari's dream of gold was shattered. Unaccustomed to the city's high altitude, he began cramping early on in the race, but managed to stick close to the leaders. Then, as runners jockeyed for position near the 11-mile marker, he collided with another athlete. Akhwari fell hard to the pavement, dislocating his knee and hitting his shoulder and head. Badly bleeding, he picked himself up and continued running.

Akhwari was the last out of the 57 competitors (18 dropped out) to finish. And even though there were only a few thousand people left in the stands, he crossed the finish line to a standing ovation. When interviewed the next day as to why he continued to run so badly injured with no chance of winning, he answered, "My country did not send me 5,000 miles to start the race; they sent me 5,000 miles to finish the race."

Stephen Akhwari was a competitor because he knew he wasn't in the Olympics to start a race, but to finish it. The apostle Paul was also a competitor because he realized that God did not have him on earth merely to start his spiritual race, but to fight, to finish and to keep the faith in the middle of it.

Jesus served as our ultimate example of a competitor, knowing His purpose wasn't to just begin his race of redeeming all mankind, but to complete it at the cross by saying, "It is finished" (John 19:30). As Christian athletes, we are also called to finish every race we run, whether in our sport or in life. No matter how badly we are beaten down or injured, through Christ's strength we can persevere and cross any finish line set before us. —*Sarah Roberts*

Go

1. Have you ever been tempted to quit? If so, what was the outcome?
2. Like Paul, how can you keep the faith?
3. What are some areas in your life that God's calling you to finish strong?

Workout

2 Corinthians 8:11; Philippians 4:13

Overtime

*Lord, help me to finish the races that You have set before me.
I look to You for guidance, strength and courage in all that
I do and say. Amen.*

Journal

Impacting the World for Christ Through Sports

FELLOWSHIP OF CHRISTIAN ATHLETES

Since 1954, the Fellowship of Christian Athletes has challenged athletes and coaches to impact the world for Jesus Christ. FCA is cultivating Christian principles in local communities nationwide by encouraging, equipping and empowering others to serve as examples and make a difference. Reaching more than 2 million people annually on the professional, college, high school, junior high and youth levels. Through FCA's Four Cs of Ministry—coaches, campus, camps, and community—and the shared passion for athletics and faith, lives are changed for current and future generations.

FCA'S FOUR Cs OF MINISTRY

Coaches: Coaches are the heart of FCA. Our role is to minister to them by encouraging and equipping them to know and serve Christ. FCA ministers to coaches through Bible studies, prayer support, discipleship and mentoring, resources, outreach events and retreats. FCA values coaches, first for who they are, and for what God has created them to do.

Campus: The Campus Ministry is initiated and led by student-athletes and coaches on junior high, high school, and college campuses. The Campus Ministry types—Huddles, Team Bible Studies, Chaplain Programs and Coaches Bible Studies—are effective ways to establish FCA ministry presence, as well as outreach events such as One Way 2 Play–Drug Free programs, school assemblies and Fields of Faith.

Camp: Camp is a time of "inspiration and perspiration" for coaches and athletes to reach their potential by offering comprehensive athletic, spiritual and leadership training. FCA offers seven types of camps: Sports Camps, Leadership Camps, Coaches Camps, Power Camps, Partnership Camps, Team Camps and International Camps.

Community: FCA has ministries that reach the community through partnerships with local churches, businesses, parents and volunteers. These ministries not only reach out to the community, but also allow the community to invest in athletes and coaches. Non-school-based sports, adult ministries, youth sports, FCA Teams, clinics, resources and professional athlete ministries are the areas of Community Ministry.

VISION

To see the world impacted for Jesus Christ through the influence of coaches and athletes.

MISSION

To present to coaches and athletes, and all whom they influence, the challenge and adventure of receiving Jesus Christ as Savior and Lord, serving Him in their relationships and in the fellowship of the Church.

VALUES
Integrity • Serving • Teamwork • Excellence

Fellowship of Christian Athletes
8701 Leeds Road • Kansas City, MO 64129
www.fca.org • fca@fca.org • 1-800-289-0909
COMPETITORS FOR CHRIST

FELLOWSHIP OF CHRISTIAN ATHLETES
THE COACH'S MANDATE

Pray as though nothing of eternal value is going
to happen in my athletes' lives unless God does it.

Prepare each practice and game as giving "my utmost for His highest."

Seek not to be served by my athletes for personal gain, but seek
to serve them as Christ served the church.

Be satisfied not with producing a good record, but with producing good athletes.

Attend carefully to my private and public walk with God, knowing that the
athlete will never rise to a standard higher than that being lived by the coach.

Exalt Christ in my coaching, trusting the Lord will then draw athletes to Himself.

Desire to have a growing hunger for God's Word, for personal
obedience, for fruit of the spirit and for saltiness in competition.

Depend solely upon God for transformation—one athlete at a time.

Preach Christ's word in a Christ-like demeanor, on and off the field of competition.

Recognize that it is impossible to bring glory to both myself
and Christ at the same time.

Allow my coaching to exude the fruit of the Spirit,
thus producing Christ-like athletes.

Trust God to produce in my athletes His chosen purposes,
regardless of whether the wins are readily visible.

Coach with humble gratitude, as one privileged to be God's coach.

FELLOWSHIP OF
CHRISTIAN ATHLETES

FELLOWSHIP OF CHRISTIAN ATHLETES COMPETITOR'S CREED

I am a Christian first and last.
I am created in the likeness of God Almighty to bring Him glory.
I am a member of Team Jesus Christ.
I wear the colors of the cross.

I am a Competitor now and forever.
I am made to strive, to strain, to stretch and to succeed in the arena of competition.
I am a Christian Competitor and as such, I face my challenger with the face of Christ.

I do not trust in myself.
I do not boast in my abilities or believe in my own strength.
I rely solely on the power of God.
I compete for the pleasure of my Heavenly Father, the honor
of Christ and the reputation of the Holy Spirit.

My attitude on and off the field is above reproach—my conduct beyond criticism.
Whether I am preparing, practicing or playing,
I submit to God's authority and those He has put over me.
I respect my coaches, officials, teammates, and competitors out of respect for the Lord.

My body is the temple of Jesus Christ.
I protect it from within and without.
Nothing enters my body that does not honor the Living God.
My sweat is an offering to my Master. My soreness is a sacrifice to my Savior.

I give my all—all the time.
I do not give up. I do not give in. I do not give out.
I am the Lord's warrior—a competitor by conviction and a disciple of determination.
I am confident beyond reason because my confidence lies in Christ.
The results of my effort must result in His glory.

Let the competition begin.
Let the glory be God's.

Sign the Creed • Go to www.fca.org
© 2013 FCA

Have You Had Your Daily Workout?

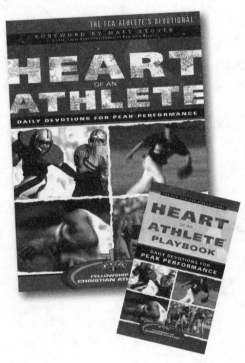

As an athlete with a passion for sports, you have a unique view of life through a competitive lens. Yet your drive for success and commitment to your sport may lead to you being set apart from others and distancing yourself from friends, family, church and school. God doesn't intend for you to go it alone. He wants to be included in your athletics and in every other area of your life. *Heart of an Athlete*™ and *Heart of an Athlete*™ *Playbook* make it easy to receive regular spiritual training that won't take over your workout schedule. Written from a competitor's point of view, they will motivate you to dig deeper into the Bible as you work through the PRESS method—Pray, Read, Examine, Summarize and Share. Now you can gain insight into handling daily challenges and using biblical principles to become a true competitor for Christ.

Heart of an Athlete
The FCA Athlete's Devotional
ISBN 978-0-8307-3850-2
ISBN 0-8307-3850-9

Heart of an Athlete Playbook
ISBN 978-0-8307-6420-4
ISBN 0-8307-6420-8

Are You Equipped to Lead Your Team?

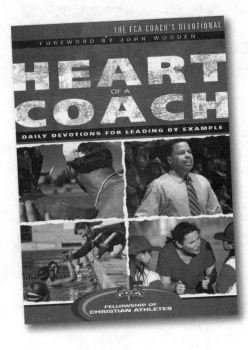

Your busy life as a coach leaves little time to read the Bible or spend time in community with other believers. And yet the need for spiritual input for yourself and those you lead is great. Since you can't give away what you yourself don't have, it is vitally important that you spend regular time with God. *Heart of a Coach™* makes it easy to receive spiritual training via short and meaningful times in God's Word. Written by current and former coaches, these 90 devotions use realistic coaching situations with Scripture references and follow-up questions to speak into your life. Issues addressed include character, faithfulness, persistence and commitment. Now you can deepen your relationship with Christ while also modeling biblical integrity to the players on your team.

Heart of a Coach
The Fellowship of Christian Athletes
ISBN 978-0-8307-3851-9
ISBN 0-8307-3851-7

COACH WOODEN'S LEGACY LIVES ON

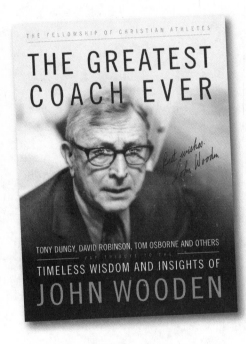

The Greatest Coach Ever
The Fellowship of Christian Athletes
ISBN 978-0-8307-5540-0
ISBN 0-8307-5540-3

Coach John Wooden's teams at UCLA won a record 10 NCAA men's basketball championships, *Sporting News* magazine named him the Greatest Coach of All Time, and ESPN honored him as the Greatest Coach of the Twentieth Century. Today, after his passing, his wisdom—capsulized so clearly in his famous Pyramid of Success™—continues to guide new generations of athletes, coaches and people of all walks of life. Yet while Coach Wooden appreciated the tributes and the honor of being called the greatest coach ever, he felt uncomfortable with the title. He was eager to see that this book points to Jesus Christ, the One whom he called the greatest coach ever. Assembled by The Fellowship of Christian Athletes, *The Greatest Coach Ever* features 40 tributes from athletes, coaches and other influential leaders that pay honor to Coach Wooden and reflect on how his example has challenged and changed their lives. Their stories can challenge and change your life as well.